ON ASSISTED
SUICIDE

ON ASSISTED SUICIDE

STEPHANIE GRAY CONNORS

THE *Dignity* SERIES

WORD on FIRE.

Published by Word on Fire, Elk Grove Village, IL 60007
© 2024 by Stephanie Gray Connors
Printed in Italy
All rights reserved

Cover design and interior art direction by Nicolas Fredrickson;
typesetting by Marlene Burrell

ISBN: 978-1-68578-135-4

Library of Congress Control Number: 2024931223

To my beloved husband Joe—
"God blessed the broken road that led me straight to you."

Contents

Series Introduction

Why dignity? Because human dignity (*dignitas*, the worthiness of each person) is the foundation of all human society. Jacques Maritain, the Catholic philosopher who helped draft the United Nations Declaration of Human Rights, affirmed this in saying, "The privilege connected with the dignity of the person is inalienable, and human life involves a sacred right."

In a time of political polarization, social division, and the ongoing "culture wars," the Dignity Series aims to refocus our attention on human dignity. The series enters into the great mystery of human life with wonder and reverence, and unflinchingly faces grave threats to human dignity, many of them ignored in the culture today.

Each volume in the series will examine one of those threats, drawing on rational argument, spiritual sources, and above all, personal stories that take readers into the lived experience on the frontier of the issue. This broad mix of ideas and approaches acknowledges that a wide variety of backgrounds and personalities shape how we interact with these questions—and that if a book is to help us grow, it has to stir our hearts as well as activate our minds.

The Dignity Series emerges out of and points back to the whole-life ethic of Catholic social teaching, which is grounded in the principle of human dignity. "Social justice," the *Catechism of the Catholic Church* teaches, "can be obtained only in respecting the transcendent dignity of man" (CCC 1929). And that dignity, on the Catholic reading, can only finally rest on our status as creatures made in the image and likeness of God (Gen. 1:26). However, these books are for anyone—Catholic or non-Catholic, religious or nonreligious—who wrestles with these issues and longs to see a more informed and considerate approach to them.

To see a full list of titles in the Dignity Series, please visit www.wordonfire.org/dignity.

Introduction

It happened back in 2015, but I remember it like it was yesterday.

It was late May, and it had been sunny and warm. It was my favorite time of day: "Golden Sunlight," as one of my photographer-friends refers to it, the best natural lighting for taking pictures outdoors. I was in my favorite city—Vancouver—which is also my birthplace and has been my home at various points in adulthood. Vancouver is situated along the coast of the province in which the license plates say "*Beautiful* British Columbia" for a reason. I was at one of the most stunning parts of the city, the peninsula on which rests my alma mater, the University of British Columbia. There are many lookouts for your eyes to feast on the breathtaking scene of vast ocean becoming one with the ever-changing sky. The sun was setting, and it was simply gorgeous out. But as I sat in the car with my fiancé, the darkest season of my life was about to begin.

Our engagement had just come to an end, and so did, it felt like, the dream of a lifetime. A purchased dress would remain unworn. A ring finger would no longer display glittering diamonds that indicated the wearer was *chosen*. But most significant of all, a heart that had finally fallen in love would now endure a death-like loss. As I left his car to sit in mine, I remember beginning to cry. Wail is more like it. From the depths of my being the suffering—the anguish—was so profound that I sounded like an animal caught in a trap. I felt utterly crushed. Decimated. Hopeless.

I called my sister and my cousin, and I remember exactly what I said to them:

"I don't want to live. I want to die."

My cousin picked me up and my sister drove to meet us. My car was left behind, and that, in a sense, was a metaphor for what I was experiencing—the power of mobility trapped in a stationary state. Heaviness. Abandonment. But the response of my family members, the literal picking up, would also act as a metaphor for how I was to eventually find healing—to be lifted, carried, connected, and surrounded.

Suffering takes all forms. For the person who wants to be married, it appears as a broken heart or an unfulfilled desire for romantic relationship. For the person who wants children, it presents as an empty womb or empty arms. For the person who wants to walk, it presents as paralysis, broken legs, or even no legs at all. For the person who wants to see, it presents as blindness. For the person who wants a job, it presents as unemployment and mounting debt. For the person who wants to feel comfort or even just "normal," it presents as chronic pain. This list could go on.

Each experience is so different, and yet there is a common thread to them all: a wish that is not, and maybe cannot, be fulfilled. A deep longing that is temporarily, or even permanently, going to be unmet. And the clash of what one wants and what one has creates the explosive force that we call suffering.

Suffering is part of the human experience. It cannot be avoided. But it can be shared. And it is when we share it, when we enter into it, when we wrestle and do battle with it, when we respond to it with creativity, that we begin to discover the power of suffering—not just in the crushing, but also in the rebuilding, the drawing in, and the uniting. This makes me think of a song by Hillsong Worship: "In the crushing, in the pressing, you are making new wine."

Over the two decades of my public speaking and writing career, I have continually declared that we should alleviate suffering without eliminating the sufferer. As time passes, I am more convinced than ever of the truthfulness of that statement—not simply that we *should* do this, but that we actually *can* do it. But note this important distinction: to alleviate suffering is not to eradicate it. I do not think we can entirely eradicate suffering from the profoundly broken and imperfect world we live in. We can certainly try, but if we fail, we must remember that there is still hope—and that the hope lies in *alleviating* suffering; it lies in bringing beauty from ashes; it lies in living for the world to come.

The importance of alleviating suffering without eliminating sufferers is so needed in a world where suicide is on the rise, where there is a segment of the population whose suffering is so overwhelming that death seems better than life.

When I was a child, I remember being taught at school about suicide. I remember being told that suicidal ideation was one secret we shouldn't keep—that if a friend expressed that she (or he) was thinking about killing herself, we should get help. I was taught that we needed to make sure our friends were safe, cared for, and protected from self-harm.

A quick Google search of "I'm suicidal" provides results leading people to resources offering suicide prevention. Advertisements with messages of support for people in such distress are in bathrooms, schools, and, as I've noticed in my travels, even in airports.

So many have been personally touched by suicide. A couple decades ago, the dad of one of my friends committed suicide. About ten years ago, a friend I knew from my university days committed suicide. And as I write this, one of my friend's uncles committed suicide. When suicide happens, people grieve. When famous people die by suicide, whether it be Naomi Judd, Robin Williams, Kate Spade, or Anthony Bourdain (to name a few), the world responds with sorrow. When the news reports on suicide, whether with headlines like "Why US Suicide Rate Is on the Rise" from the BBC or "Suicide Rates Sharply Increase Among Girls" from *Forbes* or "Suicide Deaths Reached a Record High in the US in 2022, Provisional Data Shows" from CNN, suicide is presented as a bad—not a good—thing. Typically, at the bottom of news stories about suicide, there is a message to readers to seek help if they are suicidal.

And yet, there is an interesting dichotomy occurring: while society generally decries suicide, there is an increasing acceptance of it when the word "assisted" is placed in front.

Assisted suicide (and its close cousin euthanasia) is being legalized or at the very least debated throughout much of the world. With varying parameters, restrictions, and labels (such as Canada's term of "medical assistance in dying"), getting assistance with one's intentionally inflicted death is becoming legal, or at least not punishable, in more and more places. In my home country of Canada, Parliament enacted a law in 2016 that allows for some suicide assistance. Other places where people can access that include the Netherlands, Switzerland, Belgium, Luxembourg, Germany, and Spain. Although the entirety of the US does not allow for it, a growing number of states do, including Oregon, Washington, Hawaii, California, Montana, Colorado, New Mexico, New Jersey, Maine, and Vermont, as well as the nation's capital.

Whether someone solicits another to provide a life-ending substance that he administers himself, or whether he asks another to administer a life-ending substance for him, the end result is the same: someone dies because he expressed a wish to, and another party assists him in some way in achieving his stated goal. Whereas suicide happens in isolation, assisted suicide involves another's participation.

And that leads to the topic of this book: Should suicide ever be assisted? When one no longer wishes to live, and asks another to help him end his life, what is the right response?

If suicide is wrong and if homicide is wrong, then wouldn't uniting the two in a situation where you have a type of suicide/homicide be just as wrong? When it comes to profound suffering, some people wrestle with that, and so this book relies on the vehicle of storytelling to provide the narrative on the other side of the argument that is typically not heard.

Why stories? Stories are a powerful means through which principles are demonstrated. That's why major world religions—from Judaism to Christianity, from Islam to Sikhism, from Hinduism to Buddhism—make stories a core part of their teachings. In some sense it's as though learning-by-storytelling is built into our nature, starting with young children who delight in having stories read to them. This fascination with stories never really leaves us and can be seen in adults' interest in movies, novels, magazines, and even social media—all avenues through which stories are told.

Stories captivate the imagination and engage the mind. They also are a way of sharing one's subjective experience. And that is where storytelling to defend a position on an issue can be tricky. Whenever you rely on a story to make a point, there is a risk that someone who holds an alternate view will dismiss the story as a subjective experience and argue for an alternative point using a different story. One subjective experience can seem to cancel out the other, leaving both parties no further down the road in bolstering one's position.

But sharing stories can be more than retelling a subjective experience. When objective principles are identified, they are more readily embraced when inserted *into* a story. In this case, the story does not become the argument. The story is merely the vehicle through which the argument is made clear. It becomes the means to help the mind comprehend the lesson.

Consider, for example, *Aesop's Fables*. In the story about the wind and the sun, the point is this: "Gentleness and kind persuasion win where force and bluster fail." Then, a story—namely, a fable about the wind and the sun debating about which of them can convince a man walking down the road to remove his coat—is built around that principle. The wind believes blowing hard will do so, but rather than blowing the coat off, it results in the man holding his coat close. The sun, however, quietly, calmly, and gradually comes out from behind the clouds, and as its warm temperatures heat up the environment, the man removes his coat.

When it comes to assisted suicide, this book suggests ten principles that should guide our thinking on the topic. It then draws on various stories to make those points abundantly clear and easily embraced. If followed, these guideposts will lead to human flourishing.

Start by Asking "What?"

Matt Hampson and Dan James had many things in common. They were close in age, being born within a year of each other. They both hailed from England. They were both promising rugby players. And when the men were in their early twenties, they were in separate scrummage accidents, and they both became paralyzed.

As a result of this, they both suffered profoundly. Today, Matt has turned that suffering into a source of meaning. He started the Matt Hampson Foundation to help people who have been catastrophically hurt in sporting accidents. Through his foundation, Matt was instrumental in developing the Get Busy Living Centre, where people with injuries come to get rehabilitation, encouragement, and community. He is a mentor, motivational speaker, and writer. He does all of this while using a wheelchair and a ventilator.

When Matt gave a TEDxLeicester talk, he concluded it by saying, "We can get busy living, or get busy dying. And I've decided to get busy living." Matt's focus on life, on the positive contribution he can make, aligns with this scriptural advice from Philippians 4:8: "Whatever is true, whatever is honorable, whatever is just, whatever is pure, whatever is pleasing, whatever is commendable, if there is any excellence and if there is anything worthy of praise, think about these things."

While Matt got busy living, Dan, tragically, got busy dying. After his injuries, Dan was so overwhelmed that he attempted suicide multiple times. This culminated in him traveling to Switzerland in 2008, where, at the age of twenty-three, he went to a clinic and was provided a lethal drink that he consumed.

There is no denying that a life of paralysis is a cross of tremendous weight to bear. If you are a quadriplegic, you cannot feed yourself, turn yourself, or toilet yourself. If you are dependent on a ventilator, you cannot even breathe on your own. Secondary complications from paralysis can include bladder and bowel issues, deep vein thrombosis, sepsis, pressure sores, spasticity, and more. These realities point not only to physical suffering but to emotional suffering as well, since they lead to losing independence as one knew it, relying on others for deeply personal and private care. This can feel incredibly difficult, even producing feelings of shame or worthlessness. One might also experience deep spiritual suffering, wrestling with the question of "Why me?"

If it is fair to say both Dan and Matt suffered greatly in their paralyzed states, what explains the different responses of these men? I believe the answer lies in the insight of psychiatrist and Holocaust survivor Dr. Viktor Frankl, who not only had experience guiding those who suffered but also endured profound personal suffering himself. In a recorded interview, Dr. Frankl remarked that "despair is suffering without meaning." He captured the concept with the following mathematical equation: $D = S - M$. His point was that S (suffering) is a reality of the human experience. But whether someone despairs (D) in light of suffering is entirely dependent on whether they find meaning (M). To the extent that they find meaning in their suffering, despair goes down. But to the extent that they do not find meaning in their suffering, despair goes up. And it is despair that can lead to suicide.

Finding meaning is possible even when the situation is bleak. Dr. Frankl cites a teenager in Texas who became a quadriplegic yet did not despair as others in her situation (like Dan) have. What set this young woman apart was not her experience of suffering but her response to it. She spent her days reading newspapers and watching television for an important purpose: when there was a story about someone experiencing difficult and challenging times, she would have a stick placed in her mouth so she could use it to press keys to type out letters of encouragement, consolation, and hope to them. She turned her experience of suffering into a springboard to reach out to others; it enabled her to have empathy and share hope. In short, she found meaning.

Or take another person with quadriplegia, a young man who became paralyzed at seventeen years old. Dr. Frankl received a letter from him: "I broke my neck but it did not break me." Why, like the aforementioned young woman, did this man not despair? Because he found meaning in his situation: he decided to become a psychologist, realizing that what he experienced would help him connect with and aid patients.

When speaking of people like these two young adults, Dr. Frankl said, "They can mold . . . their predicament into an accomplishment on the human level; they can turn their tragedies into a personal triumph. But they must know for what—what should I do with it?"

The key word there is "what." Whereas bestselling author Simon Sinek teaches people to "start with why," one could say that suffering can teach people to "start with what." It teaches people to ask, "What can I do in light of this? What good can I draw from it?" Of course, suffering people are tempted to start with why, asking questions like "Why did this happen to me?" and "Why must I go through this?" In fact, in his TEDx talk, Matt spoke about going through the stage of asking himself "the whys." But when terribly profound suffering happens to one and not others, "Why me?" is not easily answered. When news headlines tell us about people kidnapped and tortured, about children turned into sex slaves, about people victimized by genocide, the question "Why?" leaves us feeling empty-handed. Sure, we might say it's because we live in an imperfect world, because evil exists, or because life isn't fair, but does that satisfy?

The inability to adequately explain or be satisfied by "Why?" can leave us feeling more frustrated, adding an additional suffering to the preexisting suffering. There is an element of mystery involved. But when we accept that mystery and ask "What?"—*What* can I do now? *What* can I do because of this? *What* good can I draw from it?—then we get answers. Then we get empowerment. Then we get transformation. Making our "what" something positive that comes in direct response to a suffering that is negative does not suddenly transform the negative into something that is good in and of itself. It does not make a case *for* suffering. Instead, what it does do is make a case for bringing good *out of* suffering.

It is worth emphasizing that when good comes out of suffering, that good does not make the original suffering good. For example, imagine a woman is raped, gets pregnant, and the resulting child grows up to find the cure for cancer. It is an incredible good that an unrepeatable and irreplaceable individual accomplished such a wonderful thing. But that good fruit does not make the original rape (and the untold suffering the mother experienced) a good thing. The end does not justify the means, and so if we had a magical power to go back in history and prevent the rape from happening, we should do that. We could never justify committing evil (rape) just to bring about a good (conceive a human who will discover the cure for cancer). However, no such ability to undo the past exists. We cannot undo the evil and suffering that occurred. Since we are only left with the present and the future, we can choose to do good *in response to* bad things from the past.

And so, when anyone in a situation of profound suffering is tempted to ask "Why?" we should lead them to this insight: "Maybe you're starting with the wrong question. Maybe the question shouldn't be 'Why?' Maybe the question should be 'What?' Maybe the question should be 'What am I going to do about this?' Maybe the question should be 'What marvelous, amazing, wonderful thing am I going to create in response to this terrible, horrific, awful thing?' Maybe the question shouldn't be so much about the reason for the past ('Why did that happen?') as it should be about a response for the future ('What's next?')."

"What now?" or "What good can I do in light of this?" is a question Patrick John Hughes asked himself. In March 1988, when his son Patrick Henry was born, the exciting news of "It's a boy!" was met with a series of negative news: That boy had no eyes. He had scoliosis. He had an inability to straighten his arms and legs, which would mean life in a wheelchair. Patrick John and his wife experienced understandable suffering that accompanies an unwell child and dashed dreams. Active sports like baseball would not be a part of their father-son relationship. There were so many things that Patrick Henry would never do. Patrick John and his wife naturally asked themselves "Why?" but eventually they shifted to "What?": What can we do in response to this unexpected reality? In a short matter of time, it became obvious that Patrick Henry was a musical prodigy. At only nine months old, he began playing piano, and today, having never seen a note, he is an accomplished pianist, singer, and trumpet player.

Patrick John and Patrick Henry are an inspiring father-son duo. When Patrick Henry got the opportunity to play trumpet in the University of Louisville Cardinal Marching Band, it was his father who pushed him in his wheelchair so he could "march" along. When Patrick Henry attended university, it was his father who accompanied him to classes. When Patrick wrote a book, it was his father who coauthored it with him.

There is much Patrick Henry cannot do, and that can be cause for suffering. But there is much he *can* do, and that is where he stays focused.

The Lord of the Rings even "starts with what." In the first film, Frodo says to the wise wizard Gandalf, "I wish the Ring had never come to me. I wish none of this had happened." And Gandalf replies, "So do all who live to see such times, but that is not for them to decide. All we have to decide is *what* to do with the time that is given to us."

"What now?" and "What good can I do in light of this?" are questions Michael Morton asked himself. There aren't words to fully capture the cruel suffering Michael endured for over two decades. It all began in 1986, when his beloved wife, Christine, was brutally murdered. As if that weren't bad enough, their three-year-old son was home when the murder occurred. It gets even worse. Within weeks, Michael was arrested for murdering his wife and sentenced to life in prison—except he did not commit the crime. For almost twenty-five long, agonizing, brutal years (or, as Michael puts it, 8,980 days), Michael was robbed of his freedom through unjust incarceration.

Not only was he grieving the loss of his wife in a prison cell, ripped away from raising his son, and left with a destroyed reputation; he was also forced to live with some of the worst criminals, fearing beatings, rapes, and even murder from other prisoners. Michael spent time doing backbreaking labor under blazing Texas heat in fields amidst fire ants, mosquitos, snakes, and alligators. He endured freezing temperatures indoors during winter and overwhelmingly hot temperatures indoors during summer.

So much suffering, for so long. Why did such misery happen to Michael? Why him? How far does answering those questions get us? But *what* could he do about it? There we have answers; in fact, Michael chose a series of positive "whats" in response: he spent time in the prison library, studying case law and how appeals worked; he participated in a prison book club; he completed his college education from jail, majoring in psychology, and later pursued graduate studies from a different prison; he jogged and lifted weights; he journaled his experiences; he wrote arguments for his innocence and even composed short stories (some of which were published in small magazines).

When his case was eventually taken on by the Innocence Project, an organization that works to exonerate the wrongly convicted, their brilliant efforts and DNA-testing technology identified the actual murderer and freed Michael in 2011.

Even though his suffering of unjust imprisonment was lifted, Michael continued with a focus on what he could do as a result of what he had faced. He became a public speaker before retiring. He pursued a case against prosecutor Ken Anderson for how he mishandled Michael's trial. He did this not out of revenge but out of justice. Michael wrote in his book,

> Even though I would have liked nothing better than to simply go home and begin rebuilding what was left of my life, I couldn't walk away from my case or the glaring problems it exposed. If making a difference meant spending more time in courtrooms, if it meant speaking to state lawmakers—if it meant becoming more of a public person than I had ever intended to be—I had an obligation to do it. . . . There were people just like me still in prison. If the system didn't change, there would be more in the future.

A very powerful "what" indeed.

"What now?" and "What good can I do in light of this?" are also questions my friend Lisa asked herself. Sixteen years ago, when Lisa was in her late teens, she found herself in a psychiatric ward, confined there for a month due to psychosis. She was eventually diagnosed with bipolar II disorder. Her reality of mental illness has led to all kinds of suffering, including suicidal ideation, depression, and manic episodes. And yet the word Lisa lives by is *resilience*. She has chosen to turn her deeply personal mental health struggles into a means to help and inspire others. She regularly writes a column for a newspaper, is working on her memoir, hosts a podcast, and is a public speaker on mental health. More than that, in further asking herself "What can I do in light of this?" Lisa has joined multiple groups designed to teach wellness in various ways, including by drawing on the insights of cognitive behavioral therapy. Not only has she been a student of these programs, but she has been a mentor in them too, helping others find wellness. Her days are filled with God, work, friendship, family, connection, meeting new people, music, writing, poetry, walks, and purpose. Living with the challenges of bipolar disorder is not easy; at times, it's overwhelming. And yet, as a result of it, she has become intentional about what is needed to make her thrive in light of that reality. In identifying that, she then works to help others do the same.

"What now?" and "What good can I do in light of this?" are also questions my friends Peter and Anne asked themselves. Anne lived for decades struggling with debilitating environmental allergies and Parkinson's disease. Her allergies were so severe that she had to wear an industrial gas mask. Their home had to be isolated, meaning their windows remained closed—year round. As her condition worsened, trips away—something Peter enjoyed so much—were no longer feasible. After more than ten years of these challenges, Anne was diagnosed with Parkinson's, which she endured for seventeen years.

As her ailments worsened, she focused on *what* she could do nonetheless. And her "whats" became sewing for her grandchildren, creating memory albums, cooking at home, and praying for others. She enjoyed passing time with crossword puzzles, Sudoku, and chess. And of course, the gift of time was also passed with the gift of family—the presence of her husband and visits from her children and grandchildren. Life went on, but life went on close to home. That slower-paced, housebound life of hers also became his. One day, in the spring of 2017, Peter and Anne would dance together, not at a fancy hotel ballroom, but in the simplicity of their living room, where home was simply "being with." Home was where the other was. Tragically, three days later, Anne would unexpectedly pass away, creating a void for Peter that words cannot express.

Besides the obvious emptiness in his heart, there was a whole new emptiness in his daily life, and Peter suddenly found himself with a wealth of time. And so, he asked himself *what* all the time and ability to be away from home now enabled him to do. Answering that has led to a wealth of experiences involving creativity, contribution, and connection. Peter wrote me, "I had come to know other people who were shut-ins in wheelchairs with chronic debilitating illnesses and decided that I would start visiting them regularly at home or hospital. It quickly became evident how lonely these people are (as visitors are very sparse and far in between) and are starved for conversation. Sometimes I am the only regular visitor. The visits are about 'being with, listening to, and talking to.' In reality, we are ministering to one another and new friendships are formed."

He also spent a year teaching a religion class to nine-year-olds. And he regularly ministers to homeless women who are street workers. His decision, in his pain and loneliness, to help others in their need reminds me of the words of Dr. Frankl: "The more one forgets himself—by giving himself to a cause to serve or another person to love—the more human he is."

Peter's flourishing amidst suffering continues. He helped create and participates in a men's book club and joined a Bible study.

He made a serious return to the piano with weekly lessons and daily practice of at least two hours. He also encouraged his teacher to organize social gatherings with mini recitals of amateur adult pianists, telling me, "I believe that there are many people out there who play, that the sharing of good music has great transcendental and therapeutic value, and that such informal events should be encouraged."

Those words became very real to him in a recent encounter he had. Two Jehovah's Witness ladies knocked on his door while he was practicing piano. He decided to invite them in and play Beethoven's *Für Elise* for them. They had never heard it before and were quite moved; in fact, one of them started to cry.

He wrote me, "I feel that the music, played from the heart, took them aback, yet somehow spoke to them on a level transcending their norm, especially to the one who shed tears. The experience has further consolidated the awareness of my role in this life: I am just a steward and a servant making use of my limited talents to pass on some ineffable thing far greater, a discernment in no way diminished after becoming a retired widower."

The death of one's soulmate. Chronic physical illness. Mental illness. Unjust imprisonment. Birth defects. Paralysis. These are significant sufferings. People can, and do, respond to each in a negative way. But the above stories are proof that people can, and do, respond in a positive way too. The determining factor is in "starting with what," in the search for meaning, in the search for *what* good can come from suffering.

When someone no longer wishes to live and desires assisted suicide, those around them should assist—not with suicide, but with helping the person discover their "what."

Perhaps their "what" is to empathize with another suffering soul, to become a writer, to be a listener, to teach people how to slow down and enter into the present moment, to become an advocate for finding a cure for a disease, to leave a lesson for loved ones or perhaps even strangers working in a hospital of what really matters in life, of how to surrender, of how to release control. Their "what" could simply be to teach others, by their need and total dependence, the life-changing power of vulnerability and love.

The "whats" of the people featured in this chapter are proof that it is possible to not merely survive amidst suffering but actually thrive, to discover a whole new world of opportunity, beauty, creativity, joy, and relationship—even amidst the pain, and perhaps because of it. But typically we don't discover this on our own. Typically we need to be *assisted*. So, rather than assisted suicide, we should "start with what" and seek out assisted searches for meaning.

2

If Humans Are Equal, We All Ought to Get Suicide Prevention

On March 11, 2005, two men would meet and be forever changed. Kevin Berthia and Kevin Briggs had a chance encounter at one of San Francisco's top tourist attractions: the Golden Gate Bridge. Berthia had never been before, whereas Briggs was a regular there. Neither, however, were tourists themselves. Separated by age, work, and life experience, they were brought together by one thing: suicide.

Briggs was a California Highway Patrol officer on duty at the bridge that day. Berthia showed up to jump off of it. Since childhood, Berthia had struggled with severe depression. He had a baby who was born premature, and because she had to spend eight weeks in the hospital, he was faced with a $200,000+ medical bill he could not afford. Things were so desperate financially he couldn't even pay for a Christmas present for his beloved daughter. He was overwhelmed and thought that the way out was death.

Unaware of those details, Briggs responded to a call about a possible suicide attempt. Berthia had jumped over the railing and was teetering on the ledge. A conversation began, and Briggs mostly listened as Berthia spoke for an hour and a half about all that was overwhelming him.

More than two hundred people are alive today because of Briggs' presence on the bridge. Thankfully, Berthia is one of them. Now, more than a decade since that incident, Berthia is a father to three children and a suicide prevention advocate; he has also been a presenter at TEDx.

Briggs is rightly celebrated as a hero for saving Berthia's life. Both men are rightly celebrated as heroes for now working as suicide prevention advocates.

Their story raises important questions:

- Is it good that these men work in suicide prevention?
- Would it be equally as good if they worked in suicide assistance?
- Did Briggs do something right or something wrong by stopping Berthia's suicide?
- "Who gets suicide prevention and who gets suicide assistance?"

That last question is one that authors Jonathon Van Maren and Blaise Alleyne have brought to the assisted suicide debate in their book *A Guide to Discussing Assisted Suicide*. Their point is that if someone supports assisted suicide because they believe in honoring the desire and choice of another, then the logical conclusion is that such an individual would have to support suicide assistance consistently for everyone who *wants* to die. But if we intervene in some cases, if we actively apply suicide prevention for some people —therefore overriding their desire, their choice to die—then we are showing that the issue isn't really about choice; the issue is about judgment.

In other words, if we give suicide prevention to some, if we intervene and try to stop some suicides, then that is proof we are making a judgment that a particular individual's life is worth saving —that a particular individual's choice to die is worth overriding with our conviction to help them live. Correspondingly, then, when we assist with *some* suicides, we are making a judgment that those others are not lives worth saving. Wouldn't the most equitable approach, as Alleyne and Van Maren point out, be to either support suicide assistance for everyone or suicide prevention for everyone?

The idea that everyone should equally get suicide assistance generates an almost universal visceral reaction of horror. And that's the point: it taps into our intuition that if it would be wrong to give suicide assistance to everyone, then the most equitable alternative would *not* be suicide assistance to some but rather suicide assistance to none. Van Maren and Alleyne write,

> Most people who support assisted suicide also support suicide prevention. This is The Split Position . . . [which] considers suicide and assisted suicide as totally separate topics. People who hold to this position have often never tried to reconcile their conflicting beliefs. Our goal in responding to The Split Position in conversation is to attack this cognitive dissonance—to pit their own beliefs in preventing suicide and assisting suicide against each other, and show that The Split Position is a basic human rights violation because it splits people into protected and unprotected classes. Suicidal despair is always a symptom of some other unmet need. The desire to die is changeable, suicide

prevention is a human right, suicide assistance is a human rights violation, and our moral duty to the suicidal is to prevent self-harm, never to facilitate it.

When discussing this topic, it is helpful to distinguish means from ends. The *end* of wanting someone to be pain-free is good. Whether or not the *means* to achieve that end is morally acceptable or not is entirely dependent on what the nature of the means is.

For example, wanting your child to attend university is a good end, but if the means to achieve that is the child lying about grades or you bribing the institution with money, that is not acceptable. A good end, yes, but not a good means. Analogously, then, it is possible to want someone's life to be free of suffering, but it does not follow that all means to achieve that are ethical.

Consider for a moment what is at the heart of the belief system of civil societies: human equality. When a society aims to be civil, it develops human rights doctrines that acknowledge, for example, that people are equal because of their *nature* (human) rather than because of some *feature* they possess (e.g., age, ability, ethnicity, sex, or belief, to name a few).

Consider the United Nations' "Universal Declaration of Human Rights," which was proclaimed by the UN General Assembly in 1948. It says the following: "Recognition of the inherent dignity and of the equal and inalienable rights of all members of the human family is the foundation of freedom, justice and peace in the world. . . . All human beings . . . are endowed with reason and conscience and should act towards one another in a spirit of brotherhood. . . . Everyone has the right to life, liberty and security of person."

The right to life means someone does not have a right to unjustly take another's life away. For example, someone who shoots and kills innocent bystanders in a mall has violated the victims' right to their own lives. The right to life also means that laws should be in place to protect people from such harm to their lives. For example, a police officer who shows up to the scene has the law behind him to use the amount of force necessary to stop the aggressor in order to protect more people from being shot.

Now imagine a situation where a gunman kills five people, one of whom had plans to go home and commit suicide that afternoon. Would the shooter be charged with five homicides or only four? Clearly the answer is five, because a victim's desire for death does not change the fact that their life was taken from them by a third party. Even if the gunman knew of the person's desire for suicide and even if the gunman handed over his gun to the suicidal person to commit the act himself, the provision of the gun for suicide would be considered aiding and abetting.

So it is with assisted suicide. It involves a third party aiding and abetting in taking another's life. It therefore violates the right to life.

Someone might respond by saying that assisted suicide is *justly* taking another's life away, like a police officer using force to stop a gunman. They might say it is just because the person wants it and because the person has the right to liberty. Someone might say, "If my life is mine, and I no longer want it, then I should be able to enlist someone to help me get rid of it."

First, if that statement is true, then no restrictions on assisted suicide could ever be justified, and we should give suicide assistance to all people who request it. And most, if not all, people who support assisted suicide support it with some type of parameters, thereby invalidating the claim that if "my life is mine" then I can ask someone to help me get rid of it. Second, just because someone wants something does not mean we should follow through on their request (a point elaborated on in chapter 4). Third, as addressed later in this chapter, suicide itself is objectionable; just as a gunman has no right to take my life away, I actually have no right to take my life away either. Having an *ability* to do something does not translate into a *right* to do it. Fourth, assisted suicide is in no way analogous to justly taking a life, as in the case of using force to stop an aggressor. In the gunman scenario, someone is being *stopped* from taking life. With assisted suicide, someone is being *supported* in taking life. In the gunman scenario, precisely because life is so important, it is defended and protected; the preservation of life is paramount. With assisted suicide, life is *not* preserved, defended, or protected.

Nonetheless, in trying to justify assisted suicide, some have gone through mental gymnastics and claimed that their "right to die" is actually a part of having a right to life. The argument goes like this: If someone is not legally allowed to enlist another person to help him commit *assisted* suicide, then his only choice is suicide itself. If that person currently enjoys his life but fears that his disability or illness, when it progresses, will prevent him from committing suicide in the future (perhaps he will be unable to control his limbs), then the law that forbids aiding him will "force" him to commit suicide earlier, when he's physically capable of doing so. But because he actually wants to live a little longer and not commit suicide that early, the law that denies him suicide assistance will cause him to shorten his life, thereby denying him his "right to life" during that time.

The problem with this thinking is that it creates a false dilemma: either you give the person assisted suicide later *or* he will commit suicide earlier. The reality is, there is a third option: choose to remain living. People are more likely to choose that option if we live with the "spirit of brotherhood" that the "Declaration of Human Rights" also speaks of. What is it about the familial relationship of "brotherhood" that makes it something worth modeling? It is the notion that humans are to be treated with kindness, respect, and charity. In other words, family members should not kill each other.

Consider, for a moment, the 1994 Rwandan genocide. Amid the horrifying human rights violations, one of the most horrifying was this: colleagues, neighbors, friends, and even family members were turning over and killing *each other*. It was not just a matter of strangers killing strangers (as horrific as that is). Consider the story of Rwandan genocide survivor Monica. Her Tutsi husband and six children were brutally executed by her Hutu father and brothers. They did more than attack Monica's spouse and offspring. They attacked their bond with her. They attacked their relationship. They attacked the "spirit of brotherhood" that should exist in families, let alone all of humanity.

Or consider the story of Penny Boudreau, a woman from Nova Scotia, Canada, who strangled to death her twelve-year-old daughter Carissa in 2008. The young victim's last words to the woman who birthed her were: "Mommy, don't!" There is something horrifying about her second-to-last word—"Mommy"—in the context in which it was said. That little girl's word choice was making a profound appeal: her use of the term "Mommy" was a call to the nature of who Penny was—a mom. "Mommy, don't!" was a cry that is more about the first word than the second. It's more than *Don't kill me.* It was a shriek from the very depths of her being: *Mommy! Do what mommies do!* It was a cry for the spirit of brotherhood.

To maintain a "spirit of brotherhood" is to ensure we do not kill people. Whether it is relatives, friends, neighbors, or even strangers, the idea is that we should treat each other with a familial spirit; in other words, we should care and not kill.

Someone, however, might object that if a family member wants to die due to unsolved suffering, then a spirit of brotherhood might involve killing—*if* killing would give comfort and take away pain.

Whereas Monica from Rwanda or Carissa from Canada experienced betrayal from loved ones, is it possible that some familial killing would not be a betrayal but instead an act of mercy? After all, consider a family dog: if a beloved pet is sick and in pain and we can no longer help via veterinary means, then we do kill it to put it out of its misery. In that case, killing the dog is considered the most loving thing to do. Likewise, someone might argue, we should generally not kill our relatives; however, if their suffering cannot be eliminated, shouldn't we "put them down" as we do beloved pets?

The short answer is that we do not treat Grandma like Buddy the dog because Grandma isn't a dog. After all, would we put Grandma's food in a bowl on the floor and tell her to crawl on her hands and knees in order to eat it? Of course not—even though we do that for Buddy. Why? Because, simply put, they are *different.*

While a pet can be a nice companion, a being to sit close to, or a creature to aid someone living with a disability, pets are not humans. Pets are not our spouses. They are not our parents or our offspring. They are not business partners. They do not govern society with us. While pets should be treated with kindness, they are not our equals. As it says in the first chapter of Genesis, "Then God said,

'Let us make humankind in our image, according to our likeness; and let them have *dominion* over the fish of the sea, and over the birds of the air, and over the cattle, and over all the wild animals of the earth, and over every creeping thing that creeps upon the earth'" (Gen. 1:26; emphasis added). Animals are subordinate to us. That is not license to be cruel to them, but it is license to treat humans differently from how we treat animals. After all, when a cat kills a mouse, we do not consider it a homicide worthy of investigation, but when a human kills a human, we do.

Jesus commands us to love our neighbors, and even our enemies (Matt. 22:39, 5:44). It is our fellow humans who image God, and it is therefore not the prerogative for the creature to end the life of someone who bears the image of the Creator; hence the command, "You shall not kill" (Exod. 20:13 NABRE).

Moreover, when we put a pet down, we do so because their usefulness in our lives is outweighed by harms (such as poor health that cannot be corrected at all or without great expense, or because there isn't a home for them and they will be a nuisance to society, etc.). Humans, however, should not be valued from the perspective of usefulness.

Consider, for example, why slavery is wrong. Slavery treats humans as objects; it values another based on performance, on what the other can do and provide, and then uses and abuses the "product." To be against slavery is to be against treating humans as objects. To be against slavery is to be against valuing humans based on performance. To be against slavery is to see humans as subjects. To be against slavery is to value humans for who they are rather than what they do. To be against slavery is to see humans from the perspective of their *being* rather than their *doing*; it is to see them as being image-bearers, to see them as beings to love and be loved by. When family pets are alive, they do not always maintain their usefulness, but as long as family *members* are alive, they always maintain their being.

Moreover, if we say that love of a relative would compel us to commit a "mercy killing" because the relative wants her suffering to end, then we are left with the great challenge mentioned earlier: Who are we to decide which suffering gets suicide assistance and which gets suicide prevention? *All* of our loved ones will suffer, so how do we decide which suffering should lead to killing and which should lead to searching for meaning?

If the criteria for suicide assistance is merely that the person desires death, then relatives who may wish to die are not limited to kin who are elders. In fact, the news reported on a twenty-seven-year-old woman in Ontario, Canada, who has spoken publicly about her desire for assisted suicide because she is suffering from fibromyalgia, a nonfatal condition that has symptoms including widespread pain, fatigue, and cognitive difficulties. Where do we draw the line?

One might respond that the difference is that elders and the terminally ill are closer to death. First, notice how quickly one criterion for suicide assistance ("The person wants it") expands to two criteria ("Okay, it's not just that the person wants it; they also have to be suffering") and then to three ("Well, they have to want it and be suffering, but they also have to be near death"). At the end of the day, the growing list of criteria reinforces that not everyone is being considered a candidate for suicide assistance—but some are. Continually adding to the requirements shows that judgments are being made as to what justifies acting in that manner, thus emphasizing that some lives are seen as worth saving while others are not.

Second, another dilemma arises: How does one decide how close to death a person must be? Six months? Six weeks? Six days? Such a line is always arbitrary and subjective.

Third, what if the estimate is actually wrong? The father of one of my friends was told he had days left to live, but three years later, he was living back home.

Fourth, even if one's death could be accurately estimated, why would closeness to death be license for killing? In fact, if someone is so miserable that they want to die, wouldn't closeness to death be a consolation, whereas distance from death be a further suffering? By that logic, one could reasonably deny the "almost dead" assisted suicide because their wish is about to unfold naturally, whereas those furthest from death would be more suitable candidates for assisted suicide because, without it, their unmet desire for death would be too long a road. Of course, I am not actually suggesting this should be our philosophy; instead, I am exposing the flawed mindset for what it is: the use of killing to solve problems that can, and should, be addressed another way.

Fifth, when we create laws that allow for some suicide assistance, such as for those "closer" to death (whatever that means), there could be people who ask for assistance with suicide out of guilt and pressure. Elders and the terminally ill, who are less able to do all the things they once did, may feel like a burden on those around them; instead of having their worth affirmed, a society that allows for assisted suicide could be just the climate that "guilts" such vulnerable individuals into asking for it. Sure, those individuals may claim to want assisted suicide, but deep down they are asking for it out of duty, thinking they *ought to* because others have done so already. Since death is permanent, shouldn't we err on the side of caution? In other words, if we had to choose between a society that either a) deprives someone of death precisely when he wants it, or b) gives someone death before he truly wants it, which should we pick? The person being "deprived" of assisted suicide will still get death—just not at his own, personally calculated time. But the person being deprived of life will never get their life back.

Sixth, it is worth pointing out that where assisted suicide is legal, people in the medical community are the ones enlisted to execute it. Do we really believe that health care professionals, who have chosen a career aimed at curing and caring, should expand their "services" to killing? Consider a related issue that can involve the medical field in inflicting death: In 2016, *The New York Times* reported that the pharmaceutical company Pfizer "had imposed sweeping controls on the distribution of its products to ensure that none are used in lethal injections." More than twenty other drug companies had done the same. And the American Medical Association also raised concerns, stating that "requiring physicians to participate in executions violates their oath to protect lives and erodes public confidence in the medical profession." Couldn't the same be said about health care workers' involvement in assisted suicide? In other words, if the medical community should not be involved in ending guilty prisoners' lives, how much more should it not be involved in ending innocent patients' lives?

As mentioned previously, we naturally intuit the wrongness of giving suicide assistance to all people who want to die. But all of this shows the arbitrariness and difficulties involved with giving assistance to only some. That leaves us with the other equitable option: giving suicide *prevention* to all people. And so, at this point, it would perhaps be good to reflect on why suicide prevention is so important by asking the question "Why is suicide—assisted or alone—wrong?"

Suicide is wrong because it is a destructive solution to the universal human experience of suffering. It is wrong because it does not address the underlying problems that people feel are driving them to despair. It is wrong because it rejects the great good of life itself. It is wrong because it leaves a wake of brokenness for those left behind. As Sergeant Briggs writes in his book *Guardian of the Golden Gate: Protecting the Line Between Hope and Despair,* "Suicide ends one life, and it affects so many others. Jason [a young man who jumped from the bridge] ended his pain on July 22, 2013. He didn't intend it this way, but the pain for his parents was just beginning." Suicide is wrong because it denies hope. As Briggs also writes, "Hope is the single most important tool for anyone struggling with depression or mental illness—it can save lives. I've seen it happen over and over again, not just on the Bridge but in my experiences talking with people around the world."

From a faith perspective, suicide is wrong because it is a rejection of the gift of life given by our good heavenly Father. Nonetheless, someone might object by saying, "If I no longer want a gift someone gave me for my birthday several years ago, it is okay for me to get rid of it, so isn't it okay for me to choose assisted suicide and get rid of my gift of life I no longer want?"

To answer that, we need to realize the following: the gift of life we've been given is so valuable it's priceless. We're not talking about getting an article of clothing that will go out of style. Instead, imagine being given a billion dollars. It wouldn't make sense to use only a portion of it and say, "I don't want it anymore," and then proceed to burn the rest. So, too, would it be wrong to live a portion of our lives and then prematurely destroy them. If we don't understand how valuable our lives are, then our job is to eliminate our incorrect understanding as to our worth rather than eliminate our lives.

Moreover, think for a moment about the giver of the gift of life. The giver loves unconditionally and is perfect; he only wants our good. Therefore, his judgment is better than ours. He takes great joy in giving us the gift of life, knowing that it is life that is necessary to enter into a relationship of love—with him and with others. Can you imagine throwing a present in the face of a parent who lovingly gives his child a toy that will bring happiness? How, then, could we throw back in the face of an all-good God the gift of life he gave us?

To be sure, life on this earth has a natural expiration date built into it due to sin introducing death into the world. To address that briefly, let's return to the book of Genesis: "And the LORD God commanded the man, 'You may freely eat of every tree of the garden; but of the tree of the knowledge of good and evil you shall not eat, for in the day that you eat of it you shall die'" (Gen. 2:16–17). Sadly, Adam and Eve chose not to trust their loving Father's rule. They chose to disobey him; they chose to sin. And yet, even in God's disappointment with his beloved creation's betrayal, there lies within God's response an act of mercy:

> Then the LORD God said, "See, the man has become like one
> of us, knowing good and evil; and now, he might reach out his
> hand and take also from the tree of life, and eat, and live for-
> ever"—therefore the LORD God sent him forth from the garden

of Eden, to till the ground from which he was taken. He drove out the man; and at the east of the garden of Eden he placed the cherubim, and a sword flaming and turning to guard the way to the tree of life. (Gen. 3:22–24)

In what way was God's preventing Adam and Eve from eating from the tree of life an act of mercy after the fall? Since man was separated from God by his sin, if Adam and Eve ate from the tree of life and lived forever, they would have lived eternally separated from their Creator. By protecting them from living forever at that moment, God was giving them a second chance, a chance for their broken relationship to be repaired first.

That would come through Jesus, who would atone for man's sins by taking the punishment for sin—death—upon himself. Through his death and Resurrection opening the gates to heaven, man would have a chance at living forever in heavenly bliss.

So man would now be a pilgrim on a journey, living a finite existence in which God, like a lover, would pursue his beloved and try to win them back. As we are told in Revelation 21:1–4,

Then I saw a new heaven and a new earth; for the first heaven and the first earth had passed away, and the sea was no more. And I saw the holy city, the new Jerusalem, coming down out of heaven from God, prepared as a bride adorned for her husband. And I heard a loud voice from the throne saying,
    "See, the home of God is among mortals.
    He will dwell with them [as their God];
    they will be his peoples,
    and God himself will be with them [as their God];

he will wipe every tear from their eyes.
Death will be no more;
mourning and crying and pain will be no more,
for the first things have passed away."

So a new, suffering-free life awaits us. But until that next chapter comes, we should carefully reverence the gift of life that God has given us. Having said that, some might interject that if someone is suffering, they cannot "do" much with their gift, nor are they enjoying it, so what is the point?

When Viktor Frankl was imprisoned in concentration camps, he saw some suffering people with this type of attitude who rejected the gift of their lives by committing suicide. He wrote about how he decided he would not follow in their footsteps and would try to dissuade others from giving up on life.

One of his insights was this: "Love is the ultimate and the highest goal to which man can aspire. . . . *The salvation of man is through love and in love*. . . . A man who has nothing left in this world still may know bliss, be it only for a brief moment, in the contemplation of his beloved."

If there is no life, there can be no love. By respecting the gift of life, of an unknown duration, that each of us has been given, then we can love. Yes, we will love even better in eternity with God. If our Creator, however, in his wisdom, has chosen for our lives to carry on a little while longer on earth, we steward that life by loving rather than taking control and doing things our own way like Adam and Eve did.

That reminds me of an exchange Sergeant Briggs had with a man wanting to jump off the bridge. The individual was a wealthy businessman. His children went to private schools, and he had both a home and a fancy car. But hard times fell upon him, and he wasn't able to maintain that lifestyle. In despair, he went to the bridge to end his life. Sergeant Briggs asked him whether his marriage was built on material objects or love. The man responded that it was the latter. So Briggs followed it up with another question that became a game-changer: "If your wife lost her job or your child failed a class and was up here as you are, contemplating suicide, what would you say to them?"

The man's response? "I don't have to think about it. I would tell them how much I love them, how important they are in my life, and how much I would miss them."

When we embrace suicide, we remove the vehicle of our lives, which is the necessary instrument through which we give and receive love.

In Matthew 25, Jesus speaks of his return and how he will reward those who loved him through loving others. Jesus lists various examples of suffering souls, and not once does he propose killing as the solution to their suffering. On the contrary, what elicits God's acclaim is *working against* an individual's death by fixing a problem at its root and manifesting love:

> The king will say to those at his right hand, "Come, you that are blessed by my Father, inherit the kingdom prepared for you from the foundation of the world; for I was hungry and you gave me food, I was thirsty and you gave me something to drink, I was a stranger and you welcomed me, I was naked and you gave me clothing, I was sick and you took care of me, I was in prison and you visited me. . . . Just as you did it to one of the least of

these who are members of my family, you did it to me." (Matt.
25:34–36, 40)

3

Suffering Unleashes Love

In the summer of 2019, I sat down with the Grants, a family I have long admired. Their daughter Elizabeth is a couple years younger than me and has endured many crosses from a declining health condition. I never got to know the Grants well, but when I think of each person in their family who I have had brief interactions with, I have the same impression of them all: Peaceful. Calm. Quiet. Kind.

And so, it was they who came to my mind when I sat down to write this book. I did an inventory of people I know who have endured great trials, and although I didn't know much, I knew enough to ask whether theirs was a story they were willing to share.

When Mrs. Grant was six months pregnant with Elizabeth, she had a frightening premonition: as she hung the laundry one day, she was seized with a sense that the child she was carrying would have a disability. When Elizabeth was born, it did not appear the fear would become reality. Elizabeth was developing as expected—that is, until around thirteen months. She started to walk just after turning a year old but would fall down in a way her mom felt was abnormal. She stopped speaking at the age of six. Her physical condition declined so that she needed a walker, and then a wheelchair. Soon she no longer had the muscle tone to drive her own wheelchair. Today, in her late thirties, Elizabeth is entirely dependent on others for her survival.

She is tube-fed because she chokes. She cannot speak or write. She has no strength to even turn herself over in bed. And so, every night, her parents—who are in their seventies—will take turns waking up, going to her room, and turning over her 120-pound body so she does not experience discomfort and bed sores. If Elizabeth is itchy, she cannot tell anyone. If a strand of hair is stuck in her mouth to great annoyance, she cannot move it nor ask for someone to do so. She can and will cry out. Then, her parents must guess—and wait—to figure out what the problem is and try to solve it.

I asked Mr. Grant how they handle the twenty-four-hour care with limited respite. I appreciated his honesty: "We're tired," he said wearily. Their family has long been admired by many in their church as a beautiful witness of patience, endurance, and love. But that doesn't mean it has come easily. It doesn't mean they have some supernatural capacity to live their story void of the human experiences of grief, pain, and confusion at times.

One of the hardest things, he candidly admitted, is being at church and hearing a Scripture passage about people being healed. It pierces his heart. "Why not us?" he wonders. "Why isn't Elizabeth healed? Why isn't our prayer answered?"

I asked how he responds to his own questions. He quoted for me from John 6:68: "To whom can we go?" Just before this line in the Gospel of John, Jesus gives a hard teaching to his followers. He declares, "I am the living bread that came down from heaven. Whoever eats of this bread will live forever; and the bread that I will give for the life of the world is my flesh." The crowd does not take too kindly to this seemingly bizarre proclamation. The Scriptures say, "The Jews then disputed among themselves, saying, 'How can this man give us his flesh to eat?'" Jesus reiterates his claim, and two things happen. Many disciples declare, "This teaching is difficult," and even leave: "Because of this many of his disciples turned back and no longer went about with him." This became a defining moment. Jesus looked at his closest companions, the twelve Apostles, and asked, "Do you also wish to go away?" (John 6:51–67).

Suffering can similarly become a defining moment. Do we want to go away, and will we indeed do so? Mr. Grant knew his family's suffering, and the lack of healing, was their defining moment: Would they go away? And Mr. Grant responded as Simon Peter did: "Lord, to whom can we go? You have the words of eternal life. We have come to believe and know that you are the Holy One of God" (John 6:68–69).

When humans experience suffering, it can be tempting to question the greatness of God. It can be tempting to leave. But if we do, where can we go? If someone were to reject God, what is the alternative? Certainly running to Satan would be of no help. Satan made no personal sacrifices for humanity. Satan did not compose the Bible to proclaim a message of *Good* News. Satan has no interest in helping people. God delights in the creation and flourishing of humans, whereas Satan revels in the attack and destruction of humans.

One might suggest we disregard Satan—and God—entirely and say there is no higher power at all. But how does that position explain the complexities of creation? Consider a priceless painting: it doesn't just fall from the sky. As a painting requires a painter, design requires a designer. The intelligent design of nature, let alone creatures themselves, points to an intelligent designer—in other words, God. Sure, it takes faith to believe in God, but it also takes faith to believe the complexities of our world came from nothing. Since both options require faith, it makes more sense to conclude design comes from a designer rather than randomness. Of course, much more could be, and has been, said about proving the existence of God, and of Jesus as God in particular, but since that is not the purpose of this book, I leave the point there.

If the idea of "no God" is an option that is not logical, and if the idea of leaving God for Satan is an option rooted in misery, wouldn't the wisest choice be to side with the idea that there is a good and loving God who is all-knowing in a way we are not, and that there is nowhere else for us to go? And to trust that God sees what we do not? As the prophet Isaiah says, "'For my thoughts are not your thoughts, nor are your ways my ways, says the LORD. For as the heavens are higher than the earth, so are my ways higher than your ways and my thoughts than your thoughts'" (Isa. 55:8–9).

Therefore, when suffering occurs and we cannot understand how a good God would not intervene in the way we would, we can remind ourselves of the following: 1) We don't see the full picture; 2) we are creature and not Creator; 3) faith is trusting in the goodness of God, even when our present circumstances leave our minds bewildered.

Consider a child demanding something delightful to the taste buds, like candy. If the parent says no to the sweet treat, the child may throw a tantrum and feel the parent isn't loving. But what if there are things the parent knows and sees that the child cannot comprehend?

What if the parent knows that the child has a severe allergy and that a particular food choice would be harmful? What if the parent knows that the child needs to grow in self-control and discipline and that denying the object of desire is good for her overall maturity? What if the parent is saving the candy for another person who was already promised it? What if the parent *is* going to give the child candy, but the no is a "No, not right now," because the parent wants the child to be *extra delighted* when she does finally receive what she asked for?

The point is, the young child simply does not comprehend all that the mature parent comprehends. But if the parent is good, and loving, and kind, then we can at least trust that when the candy is withheld, there are good reasons. Not knowing the reasons should not cause us to conclude the parent is mean; rather, they should cause us to conclude that the child is not all-knowing.

I myself have learned this through the lived experience of suffering. In my case, it has been through miscarriage. I have six children, and the majority of them—four—have died within my body. When I miscarried my fourth child, I wrote this poem to God:

Why do you give me so many babies?
If you are just going to take them away?
Is this your test to see if like Job
From my lips "Blessed be your name" I'll say?
Is it to teach me
"Memento mori"?
Or like Lazarus dying and rising will you restore my fourth
And show your glory?

God did not raise our little Ollie to new life on earth, so my husband and I held yet another funeral and buried him alongside his siblings beneath our magnolia tree.

Then I got pregnant again. And everything was different—in a good way. The fifth pregnancy felt like it did with my daughter Violet, the one living child I birthed. I felt morning sickness. My abdomen swelled. And then came the ultrasounds. At week six, we rejoiced at a heartbeat seen and heard, something we had not experienced with our three other miscarried babies. At week eight, we saw that heartbeat again and rejoiced at the mercy of new life that showed every promise of remaining. And so we nicknamed our child Job, after that suffering soul in the Old Testament. We did so thinking of the end of his story where "the LORD restored the fortunes of Job . . . and the LORD gave Job twice as much as he had before" (Job 42:10).

A month later, at week twelve, we went for a routine prenatal checkup. The doppler could not pick up a heartbeat. Neither could an abdominal ultrasound. Or a transvaginal ultrasound. The doctor measured our baby, who looked frighteningly still on the screen. He measured seven weeks and three days. How could that be? I was twelve weeks along. And four weeks prior, little Job had measured eight weeks old, exactly as he should have at that stage. I felt pregnant the whole time. I had no bleeding or other signs of miscarriage.

We don't know why or when, but at some point between weeks eight and twelve, our sweet baby Job passed away, his shrinking size a sign of his decomposition. To describe our reaction as shock would be an understatement. We had thought everything was fine.

Several people told us they were praying—and firmly believed—that God would raise our child from the dead, that there would be a miracle. I truly believed God *could* raise our child from the dead. He did it for Lazarus. He could do it for our baby Job.

But I also knew God might choose *not* to do that.

When we returned home from the doctor's office, weak, weary, and emotionally spent, I lay down on our couch, and my eyes were immediately drawn to the plaque staring down at me from above our living room window: "Do everything for the glory of God."

The Scriptures tell us that before Jesus raised Lazarus from the dead, he said, "This illness does not lead to death; rather it is for God's glory, so that the Son of God may be glorified through it" (John 11:4). Would God perform a miracle and raise Job from the dead to show his glory? To reveal his power and grand works? To convince others through a miracle that he exists and loves us?

Maybe. But life has taught me that sometimes God shows his glory in another way, that he reveals his power in another manner. I knew it possible that God might be more focused on convincing others that he is trustworthy than in performing a specific miracle. How might he do all this? By my husband and I learning to suffer well. By us believing in his goodness, even when we do not understand. By us realizing that what matters most in this life is not any particular prayer being answered as we would like but God restoring our broken relationship with him through the death and Resurrection of Jesus Christ—the ultimate proof of his existence and love.

I think it's no accident that as my husband drove us home from that fateful doctor appointment and turned into our neighborhood, a large truck was driving toward us displaying two words across its upper windshield: "Just Jesus."

Our time on this earth is temporary. But life after death? That is forever. What matters more? Will we spend our eternity with Jesus? It is not wrong to improve our earthly life and to pray for miracles that would make our experiences here better. But if miracles are not part of our story, we need to remember that that is not the *end* of our story. Our ultimate happiness lies in "Just Jesus," in embracing a restored relationship with he who willed us into existence and who suffered for our salvation. That is why Horatio Spafford—who lost five of his children to tragic deaths—could pen these words that are still sung today:

When peace like a river attendeth my way,
When sorrows like sea-billows roll,
Whatever my lot, Thou has taught me to know;
It is well, it is well with my soul.

My own experience of no miracle in response to the suffering of losing four of my children brings to mind the wildly popular television series *The Chosen*, based on the life of Jesus. In season 3, there is a powerful scene of dialogue between Jesus and Little James, one of the Apostles. Little James is portrayed as having a physical disability that impacts his ability to walk. In his vulnerability, he shares that he is struggling watching Jesus heal people from all sorts of ailments and even being tasked by Jesus to go on mission to heal others when he himself remains unhealed. So he asks Jesus why that is the case. Jesus replies, "In the Father's will, I could heal you, right now. And you'd have a good story to tell. . . . But there are already dozens who can tell that story. . . . Think of the story that *you* have . . . if I don't heal you: to know how to proclaim that you still praise God in spite of this, to know how to focus on all that matters so much more than the body, to show people that you can be patient with your suffering here on earth because you know you'll spend eternity with no suffering."

Indeed, God shows his glory in the absence of miracles as much as he does in the presence of them.

As it should happen, the day prior to my miscarriage news, I was at the library and grabbed a book off the shelf by Eric Metaxas: *Miracles: What They Are, Why They Happen, And How They Can Change Your Life*. Before I knew how much his words would apply to me, I read these passages: "Any God who would heal one person and let another die an awful death doesn't seem to be a God anyone would want to worship. . . . Miracles seem to attest to the presence of a loving and compassionate God. . . . But . . . when miracles do *not* happen, we think the opposite is true."

Metaxas presents these points as common sentiments people believe. He then rebuts them:

> If God *always* answered our prayers as we wanted him to, those answers to our prayers could hardly be considered miraculous. They would only be part of a predictable system that we could manipulate. . . . It really makes God not God, but a "God" or a god whom *we* are ultimately able to control through our effort. . . . We who think of ourselves as his devotees are actually not worshiping him but rather a wished-for and prayed-for outcome. . . .
>
> If the goal of prayer is really to "get the results we want," we have a strange, candy-machine idea of God. . . . It puts me and

46

what I want at the center of things and again creates a God who is no God.

This approach is what I've previously called "Dead Religion," which is contrasted with what I have called "True Faith," where the relationship with God is central, and the things we *get* from him are peripheral. We can think of it this way: If a child really loves her father and knows he really loves her, she trusts him. When he gives her what she wants, she is happy and grateful. But even when he doesn't give her what she wants, she knows that he has a reason for not giving it to her, and not just any reason but a reason that has her ultimate welfare and concerns at heart.

This is a point Amber VanVickle would come to terms with. She was married with five young children, one of whom has severe cerebral palsy, another who has severe spina bifida, and a third who suffered a stroke—at the age of one. She and her husband prayed for miracles of healing that never came. Amber wrote,

> It took three of the greatest heartaches I could bear for the Lord to reveal what I had made of my faith, how I had loved him in my happiness and abandoned him in my heartache, how I had created a false identity of him. Three traumas stripped me of a love of God that was unworthy of him. A love distorted by motive: *"God please heal my son. . . . God, please heal my daughter."* Three heartbreaks that finally had me asking, "Lord, who are you? What do you want from me? How can I love you in this moment?" Three trials that brought me to my knees, where I could finally utter, "Lord, not my will, but yours."

In another article, Amber reflected,

Perhaps the Lord is telling us that his love is not measured simply in the physical, in the miracles and the healings, but perhaps even more so, in the absence of those. That his love is shown, even more deeply, in the crosses, the trials and tempests of our lives, in the seeming absence of his power and love. That God permits sorrow and suffering for the very end of drawing us into himself, for an intimacy and sharing-in that could not be achieved any other way than through a share in his passion: "You seem, Lord, to give severe trials to those who love you, but only that in the excess of their trials, they may learn the greater excess of your love."

A share in Christ's Passion. This perspective rang true when I miscarried my fifth child—within an hour of attending a Good Friday service. As blood poured forth from my body, I couldn't help but think of the blood of Christ pouring forth from the cross. As my son's flesh departed my body, I couldn't help but think of Mary at the foot of the cross, covered in the sweat, blood, and tears of the fruit of her womb. Jesus faced the cruelty of death, and my child did as well. But my child would also resurrect to the glory of eternal life because Jesus suffered for our sins, died in our place, and rose from the dead—ultimately defeating that harsh force we all will eventually face.

When Amber was interviewed about the metamorphosis of her perspective on suffering, she shared, "I used to want the longest life, you know, and perfect health and happiness, but . . . I'm so glad that this isn't all there is, and that we have heaven to wait for, and that we'll be with Jesus and that there will be no more tears and it's a joyful thought. . . . If I thought that this was all there is, that would be a sad, depressing thought. . . . This is not supposed to be heaven on earth."

As it should happen, shortly after that interview, Amber's sufferings increased: she was diagnosed with cancer. And in February 2023, she passed away at the age of forty. Weeks before she died, she posted online, "Hello All, The doctors tell us there is nothing more they can do but make me comfortable, so we are at hospice. But Drs and I have never seen eye to eye ;-). I am resigned to God's will, whatever that may be, but am also full of the hope of the Women of the Gospels, 'If I may but touch Him, I will be healed.' Whatever He wants!!"

Amber believed she *could* receive a miracle, but that belief was bookended by the most important perspective: that she was "resigned to God's will" and that she could declare, "whatever He wants." She was a true child who trusted her good Father, even when suffering surrounded her. In my own losses, I couldn't help but be inspired by her witness. I couldn't help but return to the idea of God's glory being magnified not just in miracles but in the lack of them.

Around that time, I read a reflection by Catherine Doherty, foundress of Madonna House, and I was struck by her words on the power of our wounds and our brokenness to reach others:

Today the world is full of doubting Thomases. We must show them the wounds of Christ or they will perish. They need to see them. We followers of Christ must show to the world the true face of Christ, at any price, even that of our life.

We are surrounded by living Thomases who will not believe in him until they put their fingers in his wounds, so we must show those wounds in ourselves.

How do we get those wounds? Very simply. By living the Gospel. For we who follow a crucified God must be crucified, too: on the cross of faith, love and surrender.

Amidst sadness, suffering, and pain, Amber could say, I can say, and so many others can say, "I know that God is trustworthy. I know he knows my wants and my fears, and I know he invites me to surrender to his love, even when I hurt, and even when things don't happen as I like. The hope I have in Christ is that not only does he want my good, but he is preparing a place for me in heaven that is for my good, and where there are no more tears." When we hold that perspective amidst our suffering, when we cling to it when miracles do not come our way, then we are able to show the wounds of Christ in our own lives to the doubting Thomases of our broken world. When they see and touch and believe, we then become mighty instruments to show them God's glory.

This doesn't mean walking through suffering is easy. There are times when one might feel incredibly overwhelmed. It is possible to choose to trust God while still feeling profound distress. When that is our experience, we can make God's Word our words. We can remember that even in the Scriptures there are prayers of lamentation that we can recite in order to find ways to verbalize the cry of our hearts. Then let us also remember that effective communication is a two-way street, so that when we cry out to God, we can listen for his responses and allow them to settle into our souls and become our new "heartsong":

Our Lamentations	God's Answer
"My God, my God, why have you forsaken me?" (Matt. 27:46)	"Can a woman forget her nursing child, or show no compassion for the child of her womb? Even these may forget, yet I will not forget you." (Isa. 49:15)
"Out of the depths I cry to you, O Lord. Lord, hear my voice!" (Ps. 130:1–2)	"As I was with Moses, so I will be with you; I will not fail you or forsake you." (Josh. 1:5)
"Be gracious to me, O Lord, for I am languishing; O Lord, heal me, for my bones are shaking with terror. . . . I am weary with my moaning; every night I flood my bed with tears; I drench my couch with my weeping." (Ps. 6:2, 6)	"The Lord is my shepherd, I shall not want. He makes me lie down in green pastures; he leads me beside still waters; he restores my soul." (Ps. 23:1–3)

Our Lamentations	God's Answer
"Give ear, O LORD, to my prayer; listen to my cry of supplication. In the day of trouble I call on you." (Ps. 86:6–7)	"O LORD my God, I cried to you for help, and you have healed me. O LORD, you brought up my soul from Sheol, restored me to life from among those gone down to the Pit." (Ps. 30:2–3)
"For I know my transgressions, and my sin is ever before me. Against you, you alone, have I sinned, and done what is evil in your sight." (Ps. 51:3–4)	"I will sprinkle clean water upon you, and you shall be clean from all your uncleannesses. . . . A new heart I will give you, and a new spirit I will put within you; and I will remove from your body the heart of stone and give you a heart of flesh." (Ezek. 36:25–26)
"She was deeply distressed and prayed to the LORD, and wept bitterly. . . . 'I am a woman deeply troubled.'" (1 Sam. 1:10, 15)	"Go in peace; the God of Israel grant the petition you have made to him." (1 Sam. 1:17)

Our Lamentations	God's Answer
"Will the Lord spurn forever, and never again be favorable? Has his steadfast love ceased forever? Are his promises at an end for all time? Has God forgotten to be gracious? Has he in anger shut up his compassion?" (Ps. 77:7–9)	"When you call upon me and come and pray to me, I will hear you. When you search for me, you will find me; if you seek me with all your heart, I will let you find me, says the LORD, and I will restore your fortunes." (Jer. 29:12–14)

Sometimes terrible things have a mysterious way of being blessings in disguise. Several years ago, my friend Magda was excitedly preparing to go on a trip to France. About five or six days before her flight, she threw one of her vests in the laundry and forgot her passport was in the pocket. She was devastated! More than that, she was hugely upset *at God* for permitting it. Magda rushed out to a Service Canada office to see if she could get an expedited passport (she could). Once there, she found out that France requires at least six months' passport validity for entry to the country and that her passport had had only two months left. In other words, had her passport *not* been destroyed, its impending expiration would have been discovered at the airport instead, and her long-anticipated France vacation is what would have been destroyed.

Or, to use another example, on one of my many trips, I heard a story from a woman who gave a testimony at a church I was visiting. She spoke about how, when she was pregnant, she developed complications that required she be hospitalized. During her stay, a more serious problem was discovered—one that would have left her dead had she not been in the right environment where medical personnel could immediately respond. In other words, the suffering of her pregnancy complication led her to the hospital, which is what ended up saving her life from being taken by another problem. This experience brings to mind the insight of singer-songwriter Laura Story: "What if your blessings come through raindrops? / What if your healing comes through tears? / What if a thousand sleepless nights are what it takes to know you're near? / And what if trials of this life are your mercies in disguise?"

Laura wrote that song, "Blessings," in response to her husband developing a brain tumor and facing all kinds of health and life challenges as a result. Their world was turned upside down, and their prayers for his healing were not answered as they wished.

In an interview she said, "Life is filled with things you don't expect, but the Bible tells us to respond by trusting God and continuing to worship him. . . . God has proven to be faithful. We have been truly blessed out of a circumstance that at first didn't seem like much of a blessing at all."

So if, in the face of suffering, we are not going to go away from God, if we are to trust in his goodness even when suffering itself is not good, how do we make any sense out of suffering?

I think one of the best answers to that can be found in a little booklet written by Pope St. John Paul II. In *Salvifici Doloris*, an apostolic letter "On the Christian Meaning of Human Suffering," he observes the following: "We could say that suffering . . . [is] present in order *to unleash love in the human person*, that unselfish gift of one's 'I' on behalf of other people, especially those who suffer. The world of human suffering unceasingly calls for, so to speak, another world: the world of human love; and in a certain sense man owes to suffering that unselfish love which stirs in his heart and actions."

Suffering unleashes love.

Elizabeth's suffering unleashed her family's love. Her parents, siblings, nieces, and nephews have learned to be more patient, more inclusive, and more tender. My husband's and my suffering from miscarriages also unleashed all kinds of love—from our priest, physician, family, and friends, who showered us in prayer, counsel, gifts, meals, and presence.

In 2014, the suffering of my friend Jocelyn's dad unleashed her love. I met Jocelyn in 2005 when I moved to Calgary, Alberta; she was one of my first friends in the new city and has remained a faithful one, even as geography has spread us apart. Over the next seven years of living there, Jocelyn was a true friend who shared in all kinds of adventures, highs, and lows. The year before I moved away, I started having sharp pains in my abdomen that led to two ultrasounds in one week to try to discover the problem (which, thankfully, amounted to nothing). I remember writhing in pain in bed one night while my roommate was away. Jocelyn came to the rescue and took care of me like she had a lifetime of nursing experience (except, instead, she had eighteen years' experience as a videographer for a television station). I personally felt, on a small scale, Jocelyn's nurturing nature and charism to care for the sick; and it was that which, two years later, she would bestow on a large scale on one of the most important people in her life.

In 2014, Jocelyn's dad, Normand, was nearing the end of his battle with cancer. In late August of that year, Jocelyn got a call from one of her brothers:

"I think you should come home," he said.

"Are you telling me I need to come home?" she responded, acknowledging the code language they were speaking—communicating that "Dad is near death" without actually saying it.

She got in her car, making the several-hour drive north. Her dad didn't leave the earth that weekend, so neither did Jocelyn leave her parents' farm. Instead, she would spend two months caring for her dad around the clock at the end of his life, the way he once cared for her at the beginning of hers. Taking time off work in order to be the main caregiver for her father was not something she had to think about. It was a conviction in the depths of her being. She simply *knew* that's what she would do. And she did.

Normand couldn't be left alone because he would attempt to get himself up and, if no one was there, he would fall. So Jocelyn was the primary person at his bedside for the duration of the days while her mom was primary for nights (with other family and friends being a loving presence as well). Because Jocelyn took time off work, her availability was an essential supplement to the care that her mom and siblings were already giving to her dad and was *the* reason Normand could stay at home.

And what did that consist of? Holistically attending to him with the gift of presence and unconditional love and attention. Sitting beside her sleeping father. Being in the room with him when he was awake. Helping him walk from bed to chair. Adjusting him when he was uncomfortable. Holding his hand. Pushing him outside in his wheelchair. Putting a blanket on him. Telling him she loved him. Being silent with him. Crying. Laughing. Feeding him. Providing his pills. Celebrating another birthday with him. Buttoning his sweaters. It was a series of seemingly little things that were actually huge for someone who could no longer do much for himself. Together, these made for a massive gesture of love. Jocelyn was entirely integrated into her father's days and fully attuned to his needs. Her gift of time made for a true communion of persons.

Jocelyn said, "I'm grateful that I was able to have that time with my dad, the intimacy of it, but also, I don't want to say share in the suffering but, to be present with him in that suffering, and learn from him until the end. He was still teaching me things, a lot of things, through that time. . . . He was still very present. A lot of people thought he was out of it, but he totally wasn't."

Because Jocelyn was providing such constant care, she had a keen sense of his needs and subtle communications. She could pick up on what he was trying to express in ways others couldn't, which was important for her dad. Being attuned to his life and his suffering is what made her respond with the gift of time and tender affection.

In 1962, Rick Hoyt's suffering unleashed his dad's (and mom's) love. It was that year when Rick was born. Due to being deprived of oxygen at birth, Rick was forever changed. He would live with spastic quadriplegia cerebral palsy. His parents, Dick and Judy Hoyt, vowed to care for him, showering him in love and opportunity (which included Rick working hard and getting a university degree). They rejected the recommendation that they institutionalize him.

As the years went on, Dick and Rick have partnered up for marathons, triathlons, and even Ironmans. Son sits in a wheelchair (or dinghy), and dad pushes (or pulls). Even when Dick had a heart attack, not long after his recovery he was back running with his son. Their story is all over the internet and has received millions of views, and it is a constant source of inspiration for people worldwide.

In 2013, they received the Jimmy V Perseverance Award. In his acceptance speech, Dick declared, "Rick is my inspiration. He has taught me a great many things over the years. And every day I consider myself lucky to be his father and teammate. . . . Next time you see someone in a wheelchair, or who can't talk or walk, or they may talk or walk a little bit different, they are people too, and deserve to be able to live, learn, work, and play."

Rick's acceptance speech, spoken through a computer, was a powerful indication of the fruit of someone who received love in the face of suffering: "Yes you can," he told the audience, imparting Team Hoyt's motto. "Don't give up," he quoted from the award's namesake. "Don't ever give up."

The friendship of Justin Skeesuck and Patrick Gray also demonstrates the concept of suffering unleashing love. These two men have been lifelong friends, and their brotherhood only strengthened when tragedy struck: Justin developed a progressive neuromuscular disease, and it deteriorated to the point that he now needs a wheelchair. Rather than wallowing in misery, Justin has demonstrated remarkable resilience and determination, which included fulfilling a desire to do the Camino de Santiago, known as the Way of St. James. In 2014, the men trekked the Way in a truly profound story of community, suffering, opportunity, and love. The Camino is a challenge at the best of times. Now imagine inserting a wheelchair into the picture.

I'll Push You: Embracing God's Promise of Provision is a one-hour presentation on YouTube about their journey. In it, they reveal the ripple effect of suffering unleashing love. Justin's suffering unleashed Patrick's love in his willingness to even go on the journey. Then, while traveling, they faced backbreaking suffering in the form of having to navigate all kinds of mountainous, rough, muddy terrain, and it unleashed all sorts of love from fellow pilgrims who began as strangers but became like family as they helped them on their life-changing trek.

When talking about their experience, Justin and Patrick share a powerful story of a fellow traveler named Claudia who had helped them various times over a two-week period.

Claudia's story is a reminder that everyone on the Camino carries more than a backpack; they carry a personal story that is their reason for being there. Claudia's was particularly traumatic. Only half a year prior, on December 31, 2013, she had been home with family in South Africa. They were fulfilling their New Year's Eve tradition by setting up a camera for a family photo, doing the countdown, and capturing an image at midnight. "Ten, nine, eight . . ." they shouted. But when their countdown landed at one, masked gunmen burst into their home and Claudia's dad was murdered in front of her eyes.

Needless to say, she was walking the Camino filled with great anger, pain, and confusion. In a word, she was suffering. And yet, even in her hurt, she enjoyed helping Justin, Patrick, and their ever-growing team. One day, they were working to get Justin in his wheelchair up a particularly steep cliff, and in order to unite the team's effort, Justin began a countdown: "Ten, nine, eight . . ." You can only imagine the trigger that was for poor Claudia. The numbers brought her back to the trauma of that New Year's Eve night. It was agony. She didn't want to hear those numbers. Not like that. Not again. She was suffering.

She nonetheless carried forward in helping the team push Justin. Later she journaled that upon summiting, when she and the others were joyfully celebrating their accomplishment, she was moved to tears because "I didn't believe that a countdown from 10 could ever be happy again."

Claudia recalled an exchange she had with Justin that evening, when the team was spending time together as a brilliant sunset lit up the sky: "Justin looks at me and says, 'Thanks for getting me up that hill today.' I look back at him and say, 'No, Justin, it was *you* who got me up that hill.'"

Every person, in some way, is suffering, and with that reality comes all kinds of opportunities to unleash love. Proof of this isn't only in stories told on a grand scale to the world through presentations and popular online videos. Proof of it is also found on a small scale, in our everyday lives. When I went through my broken engagement, my suffering unleashed the love of my cousin Belinda (among many others). Several weeks after my heartbreak, I left town for a five-day business trip. When I returned, I was surprised to learn that Belinda had spent that whole time completely transforming my basement suite. She knew my ex-fiancé had spent so much time visiting me that she wanted to give the place a brand-new look. She turned it into an absolute oasis that definitely could have qualified for an HGTV home makeover success story. I was suffering, and it drew out of her great love. Not only did she sacrifice her time and her money that week, but she did it all while going through a flare-up of her rheumatoid arthritis.

Or I think of a friend of mine who went through the worst postpartum depression I've ever witnessed, so severe that she had to be hospitalized a couple of times in order to get the right help. And her suffering unleashed all kinds of love, from visits to meals to money to support to counsel to babysitting to prayers—you name it—from friends, family, the medical community, and her husband, who all tirelessly rallied around her.

But the idea that suffering unleashes love is a concept that is present in more than personal stories. It is a concept at the heart of the Gospel message. Consider the Scripture passage most commonly held up on poster board at sports games: John 3:16. What does that passage say? "For God so loved the world that he gave his only Son, so that everyone who believes in him may not perish but may have eternal life."

When original sin entered the world through Adam and Eve's choice to disobey, humanity was separated from God. "For the wages of sin is death" (Rom. 6:23). God, however, did not leave us in that suffering state. In his majesty and creativity, he let our suffering unleash his love. He sent his only Son to enter into the human experience. And although Jesus was innocent, he would endure our punishment for sin. He would be tortured and killed. He would take the place for us. Then he would rise from the dead and open the gates of heaven so that we could have eternal life. Our suffering unleashed God's love. And that love restores us back to life: "The free gift of God is eternal life in Christ Jesus our Lord" (Rom. 6:23).

Instead of someone's suffering unleashing assisted suicide, what if we focused on their suffering unleashing love? That love can take all kinds of forms. It may mean holding someone's hand while listening to beautiful music. It may mean reading to them because they can no longer see. It may mean playing a board game with them. It may mean transcribing their life lessons as their legacy to leave behind. It may mean acting as interpreter to their blinking eyes, which is their only way to communicate. It may mean changing their soiled diaper. It may mean gently wiping drool off their face. It may mean doing what my friend Josh did when his grandma was dying from cancer, which had riddled her body and left her emaciated: crawling into bed and curling up next to them—a simple but powerful gesture that speaks more than words ever could, an act of pure love that communicates, "You are not alone."

In 2019, CNN's Anderson Cooper interviewed comedian Stephen Colbert. Both men lost their fathers when they were just ten years old. In Colbert's case, his dad died in a plane crash alongside two of Colbert's brothers. When speaking to Cooper about this, he said,

> What do you get from loss? You get awareness of other people's loss. Which allows you to connect with that other person. Which allows you to love more deeply. . . . And so, at a young age I suffered something so that by the time I was in serious relationships in my life, with friends, or with my wife or with my children, is that I have some understanding that everybody is suffering. And, however imperfectly, acknowledge their suffering, and to connect with them and to love them in a deep way that not only accepts that all of us suffer, but also then makes you grateful for the fact that you have suffered—so that you can know that about other people. . . . It's about the fullness of your humanity.

Consider his words in light of the Gospel, and they become even more powerful than they already are! God did not create humans and remain far removed from them. No; instead, he fully entered into the human experience by becoming man. He experienced suffering and anguish like everyone else. Just as you or I can connect with others who suffer because of our own suffering, so too does God connect with us in a profoundly personal way. Suffering to him is not just an idea; it is something he experienced through Jesus.

4

We Can Alleviate Suffering without Eliminating Sufferers

It was an encounter science predicted would never happen. As I sat sipping coffee, my interviewee, a thirty-year-old teaching assistant, enjoyed a root beer, masking the reality that he normally received nutrition by a feeding tube. But I guess root beer isn't really nutritious. I suppose if you're going to ingest it, you may as well let it serve its only purpose—to treat the taste buds.

Moe Tapp was "supposed" to be dead twenty-eight years ago. But sometimes people defy the odds. I learned about his condition two years before learning about him. Epidermolysis bullosa (EB) is something I tell my audiences about when I speak on assisted suicide and suffering. I often tell the story of Jonathan Pitre, a teenager who lived for eighteen years with the excruciatingly painful condition, and I talk about how killing people ought *not* be the solution when we need to kill pain.

And then, one day, a person with EB showed up in my audience: Moe was grateful someone was telling others about "the worst disease you've never heard of," as an EB organization describes it.

When we subsequently met at an A&W in downtown Vancouver for him to tell me his story, I reacted the way most do when they encounter someone whose skin is as fragile as a butterfly's wings, whose painful blisters cover a majority of his bandaged body: "Is it okay to hug you?" I cautiously asked, not wanting the pressure of a hug to inflict pain.

"Yes," he said. "Don't worry. If it would hurt me, trust me, I wouldn't let you." He does, though, have a fear of falling and typically needs assistance walking down stairs to ensure he doesn't fall—because he has, and there aren't words to describe the searing pain of blistered skin slamming against hard floor.

It has been said that two people can look at the exact same thing and see something totally different, which demonstrates that "perspective is everything." That is certainly true when considering Moe's story.

One could focus on Moe's bedtime routine: how he connects his feeding tube so liquid nutrients can be slowly dripped into him while he sleeps.

But it would be better to focus on what Moe wakes up for: his employment at a high school where he works with students from grades 8–12 who have learning issues of all kinds, including ADHD, dyslexia, autism, etc. His own experience of suffering, and rising above it, gives him profound compassion. He is fulfilled in being needed by his students, who are fulfilled by him connecting with them, by his belief in them and their ability to achieve.

Moe could be frustrated by the stares and questions he gets about why he looks different and whether or not he was burned in a fire or car crash. But instead he seizes the inquiries as opportunities to raise awareness about EB. As Moe said, "We won't find a cure if people don't care, and people won't care if people don't know." Moe confidently initiates discussion of his condition every year with a new crop of students. He encourages their inquisitiveness. In doing so, he not only teaches them about his condition; he teaches them how to be accepting of another's differences.

One could focus on the brief period of anger Moe went through in his mid-twenties. Blisters in his throat caused such severe pain that he couldn't eat at all by mouth. He realized then that he would never be able to be spontaneous and just go traveling without doing weeks of research to make sure he could get all that he needed in a new environment.

But it would be better to focus on the camp he went to in Minnesota, where anyone in the world who has a skin disease is invited to gather. He first went as an attendee and then returned as a volunteer. Knowing he was part of a broader community of people whose shared experience enabled them to readily empathize with each other gave him encouragement. Attendees cheered each other on with this philosophy: "If you can do this, if you can overcome, so can I."

One could spend time dwelling on the burden and pain of baths and dressing changes every two to three days that cost $1,000 a month—and the infections and exhaustion that come along with living with EB.

But it would be better to reflect on how his Catholic faith has sustained him (and become more personal and real for him in adulthood) and how his family and friends have rallied around him and stood by his side. Besides his faith, Moe is also passionate about gaming and loves watching wrestling (and dreams of being a commentator for pro wrestling). Old school rock and roll is his music genre of choice, and reading is also on his list of enjoyable activities.

Moe has never thought of suicide. But on that topic, and its close relative euthanasia, he said he does understand why people would consider these options due to pain—not that he supports them; in fact, he views both as wrong and would instead focus on pain relief and comfort. He noted that he became convinced euthanasia was wrong when he heard a compelling pro-life presentation; he realized that to say someone like him should be allowed assisted suicide but others should not is to make the judgment that his life is somehow less valuable than someone who is nondisabled. He said that if someone wanted to end their life, he would ask why, then see what their life was like at home, at school, etc., and then work to make that person's life better.

"There's hope, always hope," he declared. "I know it sounds corny, but it's true. People will always be around you that care."

Of course, if such people are lacking, it would be better to *introduce* supportive people rather than *eliminate* a suffering person. Moe himself has reached out to families whose babies are diagnosed with EB. They first connect over the condition but remain friends because of a familial bond that forms.

At the beginning of the interview, I asked Moe how he would describe himself. "Good natured," he said. "[A] good dude, pretty chill." That definitely captures my observation of him; and when I think of that, plus the full and satisfying life he leads, even with—and perhaps because of—such a debilitating condition, I think about how, in a paradoxical way, Moe Tapp is comfortable in his skin.

What's notable about Moe's story is that his pain and suffering have not been entirely eliminated; however, his joy and fulfillment in life are proof that even when we cannot eliminate suffering, we can alleviate it.

If, on the contrary, we eliminate people whose suffering we do not yet know how to fix, what motivation would we have to come up with better pain management, and so forth? My friend Dr. Will Johnston, a family physician, once wisely remarked, "When you see only death as a solution, you throw creativity out of the window. Medical diligence goes out the window. The need to actually solve the problem, the need to actually examine the patient, and find a solution, goes out the window."

Consider how different our world would be if, one hundred or more years ago, when diabetics were dying for lack of insulin, society euthanized them? There is a big difference between killing as the solution and death as the problem. With the former, we are less motivated to come up with other solutions because we have found one. But with the latter, it's the lack of solution that becomes motivation for getting creative. Indeed, people dying from diabetes became a motivating factor to develop insulin, which is a game-changer for people suffering from that condition.

Other ways of getting creative and being solution-oriented are to focus on disability supports, like home care / personal support staff, accessible housing, mobility devices, accessible transit, accommodations for sensory disabilities (audiobooks, hearing aids), and peer support.

Having said that, as much as we should work to alleviate suffering without eliminating sufferers, we cannot stave off death forever. Proponents of assisted suicide may characterize opponents of it as people who want to keep others alive on this earth forever. That is simply not true. Opponents of assisted suicide recognize that death is inevitable. It is just that we don't believe in assisted suicide or homicide as means to bring about that death; instead, we believe in letting nature take its course while offering comfort that addresses the whole person.

This is what palliative care does, which is a great alternative to assisted suicide. Consider this definition by the World Health Organization: "Palliative care is an approach that improves the quality of life of patients and their families facing the problem associated with life-threatening illness, through the prevention and relief of suffering by means of early identification and impeccable assessment and treatment of pain and other problems, physical, psychosocial and spiritual."

The point is that even when cures don't exist, comfort and quality care are possible. When we handle peoples' suffering properly, they are unlikely to request assisted suicide. Consider the words of Jean Echlin:

> With 26 years' experience as a palliative care nurse specialist and consultant, I have been at the bedside of more than one thousand dying individuals. Thus, I can assure you that persons who receive timely, appropriate and expert pain and symptom management, including attention to significant socio-spiritual, psychological and emotional issues, do not ask for assisted suicide or euthanasia. With the inclusion of family members as the "unit of care," people want to live as long as possible! In fact, good hospice/palliative care can actually extend the life span. As well, it gives patients an improved quality of life at the end of life.

An audience member taught me the truth of that statement with her lived experience. She told me about a colleague she had befriended while working at Walmart. The colleague developed spinal cancer and was in the end stages, facing excruciating pain. She was so overwhelmed by her condition that she filled out paperwork for assisted suicide. She needed a witness to sign the document and asked her friend to sign. The woman told me that she looked compassionately at her suffering friend and gently said, "I can't do that." She then sat down on her friend's bed and tenderly asked, "What are you most afraid of?" The woman said, "The pain!" She was already enduring great suffering and feared it only getting worse.

The woman asked about them consulting palliative care pain specialists to see what options were available to her as it worsened and discovered helpful interventions existed that didn't have to include suicide assistance. She promised to continue visiting her friend, and when she did, she would wrap her arms around her and give the gift of presence and touch. She knew her dying friend loved butterflies, and she would say to her, "Imagine yourself soaring with the butterflies." The dying woman said that even though she was suffering, "there are still moments of joy." Because she decided to reject suicide assistance, she experienced those moments of joy; she was helped by the medical advances of pain relief; she knew the comfort of a friend who demonstrated true compassion—"to suffer together." The friend passed away naturally within a week, knowing the loving presence of her sons and that woman who cared enough to say no to suicide assistance and to help create an alternative solution.

Instead of using the unethical means of killing to achieve the result of ending someone's suffering, the key is to surround people with consolation until death comes for them, and good palliative care makes that possible. One of my childhood best friends, Julia, became a family physician and also does some work in hospice. In a presentation to teenagers on the topic of assisted suicide, she shared,

> I think it is possible for people to have a "good" death. I think of my patients who come to the hospice when it is clear that their cancer is not going to be cured. They may choose not to have further treatment, based on the side effects. [This is an important point. Patients can still refuse interventions that are disproportionate, even if they don't believe in assisted suicide.] Once at the hospice, they have their own room. They are surrounded by their families until the end. They can accept what is happening and face it with peace, even though it is always sad to say goodbye. Nurses are present to try to ease their pain and take care of their needs. I think of the time they have talking to their loved ones. When you know that your time is limited, each conversation is more meaningful. Each moment together matters. Families will not forget those moments.

Palliative care is not easy—it requires people to be creative, like helping people redefine their goals. Sometimes if a parent has a terminal illness, this means helping them write letters to their children to be opened at specific times—like high school graduation. Even though the parent longs to be there in person, they can still be present through a meaningful letter.

Julia's remarks about patients using whatever time they have left to leave an intentional legacy for their loved ones remind me of my friend Alex, who I write about in the epilogue. Alex was a young father who died of cancer; rather than shortening his life with assisted suicide, he maximized his time by preparing for his passing until illness finally stopped the clock. His wife, Elaine, wrote,

> One of the kindest things Alex did as we started to prepare intentionally for his absence was that he gathered a group of men from family, school and church and shared with them the burdens of his heart and some of the practical needs he felt they could meet once he was gone. He gave them very concrete ways in which he wanted them to help, from assisting me with some household tasks to encouraging the children as they grew older. I can only imagine how difficult this must have been as he contemplated all the moments when he would not be there, and I was so proud of the courage and grace he showed in that moment.

Or take the insights of Dr. B.J. Miller, a hospice and palliative care physician who gave a TED talk in 2015. He remarked, "Since dying is a necessary part of life, what might we create with this fact? . . . I am asking we make space—physical, psychic room to allow life to play itself all the way out, so that rather than getting out of the way, aging and dying can become a process of crescendo through to the end."

Crescendo! As a musician, I love this illustration. When playing music, anything marked with crescendo means you are gradually to increase the volume. Too often we view death and dying as fizzling out rather than as an epic orchestral ending. Understandably, the reality of disease and dying doesn't mean people will necessarily be *showing* a crescendo externally. Death can be very hard—in fact, even brutal at times. The question is, how can we make a crescendo happen internally? We can be intentional about the environment a dying person is in by making it beautiful; we can ensure the people they are surrounded by are tender; we can make sure the conversations and reflections that occur are healing.

Dr. Miller also said, "Let death be what takes us, not lack of imagination." With assisted suicide, death doesn't take us—we take death, and when we do that, people die for lack of imagination; they die for lack of a creative response to the suffering they are facing. In contrast, palliative care is about using our imagination and getting creative. Julia addressed this when she spoke to those teenagers:

I would like to challenge each of you today to think about how you can be defenders of life. One of the most important things that sick people need is companionship. People fear abandonment even more than pain. So if you know someone who is unwell or in a hospital or nursing home—visit them. Get to know them. If you feel awkward or don't know what to say, just be present. Think about when you were a kid and your mom or dad sat by when you were sick—something about them being there was comforting. Pray for the people you visit. Read to them or listen to music with them. I think of the character in the book *Still Alice* who loves ice cream. Even as her memory fails because of dementia, she continues to enjoy the experience of eating an ice cream cone. Find out what people enjoy and make it possible.

When you're thinking about your future career, consider how you can help improve the lives of sick, disabled, or vulnerable people. This could mean working directly in health care, but the possibilities are broader than that—think of interior designers who make nursing homes more beautiful, or chefs who prepare meals for patients in a hospice, or engineers who design new equipment to keep people mobile, or administrators who organize volunteers to visit the elderly.

So we should get creative; we should replace assisted suicide with more and better palliative care. But what about some specifics? Since death is a part of life, when illness arises, how does one make ethical decisions that neither hasten nor prolong death? There are various resources that go into great depth about the nitty gritty of ethical decision-making during end-of-life care, and that is not the purpose of this book. However, I will propose a few questions to ask that highlight general principles we should keep in mind:

IS MY BEHAVIOR REFLECTIVE OF RESPECTING THE DIGNITY OF THE PERSON AND THEIR LIFE?

When deciding what treatments to begin, continue, or cease, it is important that our underlying disposition be one of seeing the patient's life as valuable, independent of their abilities or productivity. Referring to an individual as a "vegetable" or a "drain on resources" would be dehumanizing language that ought to be rejected. Our attitude should be one of seeing them as image-bearers, individuals to love and be loved by. If this is the universal starting place, then it's easier to have discussions about what interventions should or should not be made because you know all parties are working from this life-affirming foundation.

IS THE PERSON'S DESIRE ORDERED OR DISORDERED?

It does not follow, by the mere existence of a wish, that we should fulfill it. After all, what if the wish is disordered? Consider the condition body integrity identity disorder (BIID), where people with healthy body parts are convinced, in their minds, that they should be disabled in some way. (Some with BIID desire to become amputees, even though there is no presence of a pathology that would warrant amputation.) By this example, we can see that we humans have all sorts of desires; some of our desires are rightly ordered (such as, "I have gangrene and wish for my infected leg to be amputated"), and some of our desires are disordered (such as, "My body is healthy but I want my leg removed"). Wouldn't we consider it medical malpractice for a physician to fulfill the disordered desire of someone with BIID?

Correspondingly, the fact that someone expresses a desire to die doesn't mean we should follow through on it, since the desire is a disordered one. But how can we label the desire to die as disordered? Consider our natural human intuition (regardless of whether one embraces a religious worldview or not) when it comes to life and death. In 2014, there was an outbreak in Africa of the deadly virus Ebola. What did people fear? Death. What was the world's response? Preserve life.

That same year, a Malaysian airline plane was shot down and crashed over the Russia-Ukraine border, killing almost three hundred people. One Scottish couple, Barry and Izzy Sim, as well as their baby, were supposed to be on that flight but, due to overbooking, were put on another plane. What do you think their reaction was to not being on the deadly trip? Gratitude at being *alive*.

Or imagine this thought experiment: You run into an elderly friend at the grocery store who announces her first grandchild was born. Wouldn't "Congratulations! How wonderful!" easily fall off your lips? What if shortly thereafter, she lets you know that her husband was diagnosed with cancer? Wouldn't you just as quickly express sorrow and sadness? What does that tell us? We rejoice at life and are saddened by death (or the potential of death).

Animal Planet TV aired a program called *I Shouldn't Be Alive*, which documented real stories of people who got stuck in avalanches, canyons, the ocean, etc., who almost died but hung on. Captions for the series trailer were "Never Give Up" and "The Power to Protect" and "There is a strength within us all. . . . The will to survive." It demonstrates the overpowering drive to choose life and not death. Just consider rescuers who search for missing people: there is joy and elation at finding people alive and sadness and devastation when rescuers arrive too late.

Or consider those who attempt suicide. Harvard T.H. Chan School of Public Health reports that "nine out of ten people who attempt suicide and survive will not go on to die by suicide at a later date." And a majority of people (70 percent) whose suicide attempt results in medical care do not go on to attempt suicide again. This shows that a desire to die is not permanent. Take the powerful story of Kevin Hines. As a baby he endured terrible neglect and abuse at the hands of his birth parents, then faced more trauma in foster care, and while he was ultimately adopted by a loving family, in his late teens he experienced a sudden and serious onset of bipolar disorder. Within a couple years, he jumped off the Golden Gate Bridge and, remarkably, survived. He describes the moment he jumped by saying, "The millisecond my hands left the rail—instantaneous regret. What . . . did I just do? I'm going to die and I don't want to." Now Kevin is a motivational speaker and author and is internationally renowned for his anti-suicide work.

These are just a few illustrations of our human intuition of choosing life over death. Therefore, when someone says that they want to be killed, we should not follow through because such a wish is disordered. If we dig deeper, we will likely see that the disordered desire has beneath it an *ordered* one—perhaps a desire to no longer suffer or a desire to be with Jesus in heaven. Those desires are good, but killing is not.

WHEN THE PERSON DIES, IF I TRACE THEIR DEATH BACKWARD TO ITS CAUSE, WHAT WILL THE CAUSE BE?

While recognizing that there ultimately comes a time for all of us to pass away, the key is that that time should not come at the hand of another or the self but due to factors beyond our control, such as age, disability, or illness. So we can ask: Has a person died due to a condition, or were they killed (whether by omission or commission) at the hands of another? If, for example, someone has cancer and is smothered to death by a pillow, it would not be accurate to say the individual died from cancer. Nor would it be accurate to say the individual "stopped breathing." Instead, they would have died from being killed by way of oxygen deprivation intentionally inflicted by another party with the purpose of ending their life. The same is true with a euthanasia injection or pill; in such cases, the underlying disease is not what ends their time on earth, but rather the hands of another (whether the patient requested it or not).

This reality gives us an opportunity to think about how cold assisted suicide is and how much it lacks compassion—even though some try to "dress it up" with compassionate appearances by throwing parties the night before, playing peaceful classical music, or surrounding the person with loved ones. At the end of the day, in such a situation, the "moment of death" is calculated and premeditated; it is quite literally death at the hands of another person rather than the consequence of illness.

IS A PARTICULAR COURSE OF ACTION PROPORTIONATE OR DISPROPORTIONATE?

Death *will* come for each of us. So how do we determine when it is death's time and when we should continue with treatment? This is where examining whether a treatment is proportionate (or ordinary) versus disproportionate (or extraordinary) is helpful. By looking at the totality of an individual's health condition and prognosis, the interventions we have available to us, and how a particular patient's body will respond, we should ask: Will a treatment offer a reasonable hope of benefit and not be excessively burdensome (and therefore be proportionate) to the patient, or would it not offer a reasonable hope of benefit and be excessively burdensome (and therefore be disproportionate)? There is a moral duty to pursue the former but not the latter.

For example, a friend of my friend had ovarian cancer that she battled for just over two years. Initially, she pursued all kinds of treatment and medical interventions with the hopes of killing the disease invading her body. As time progressed, however, and the disease took on a life of its own, it became tragically clear that pursuing treatment would not ultimately eradicate the cancer. In fact, the aggressive interventions would bring a series of negative complications to her that would not be balanced by benefits. She reasonably ceased treatment that was clearly disproportionate in her case and was given excellent hospice care until she passed away.

Or, to give another example, during one of my presentations, a plastic surgeon who had several decades of experience as a burn specialist raised his hand during Q&A. He shared with the audience that some patients aren't saved. The reality is, there are times when a medical team ceases disproportionate interventions and a patient succumbs to the underlying condition. But, he cautioned, as a physician he rejects homicide. In no uncertain terms, he pointed out that doctors should not kill a patient. There is a significant difference between killing someone versus not being able to ward off death.

So let's consider the concepts of proportionate and disproportionate interventions as they relate to a specific case: someone who has stopped breathing. Should CPR (cardiopulmonary resuscitation) be done? That depends.

Ethicist Rev. Tadeusz Pacholczyk provides this helpful information for discernment:

> Some of the possible burdens that may need to be considered in deciding whether to pursue resuscitative interventions for a patient would include some of the following: the risk of rib or other bone fractures, puncture of the lungs by a broken bone (or from the trauma of lung compression and decompression), bleeding in the center of the chest, cerebral dysfunction or permanent brain damage. . . .

During resuscitative efforts, elderly patients are more likely to experience complications or to have ribs break during CPR. Younger patients, on the other hand, tend to show a greater resilience and are often better able to tolerate CPR. Patients suffering from advanced cancer are also known to fare poorly following resuscitative efforts.

So rather than make sweeping statements like "You should always do CPR" or "You should never do CPR," decisions are made on a case-by-case basis. This way one can consider, in light of a specific patient's condition along with an intervention's benefits and risks, whether a procedure would be proportionate or disproportionate in that moment.

ARE WE TALKING ABOUT TREATMENT OR CARE?

Contrasting treatment versus care enables us to see that some human needs are so basic that they shouldn't be classified as "treatment" (something only those with specific conditions need) but rather as "care" (something everyone needs).

Administering nutrition and hydration is an example of care, not treatment, because food and water are basic requirements for all humans to live. Absence of these can lead not only to death but also to great suffering until one dies. (Just consider your own experiences of hunger, pain, or thirst.) The general rule should therefore be to administer them.

Having said that, even care like food and water can become, for some people who are very sick and dying, disproportionate, and it would be morally acceptable to cease administering them. Let's look at some specifics. The United States Conference of Catholic

Bishops (USCCB) gives a helpful example in its literature by stating, "A patient in the last stages of stomach cancer is already dying from that condition. Such a dying patient, or others who can speak for the patient, may decide to refuse further feeding because it causes pain and gives little benefit. The administration of nutrition and hydration in this case would pose a burden on the stomach cancer patient that is disproportionate to its benefit."

Rev. Pacholczyk once again provides helpful insight on this topic:

> In some cases, feeding tubes may actually cause significant problems of their own for a patient. For example, if someone is facing an advanced illness, perhaps with partial bowel obstruction, a feeding tube can sometimes cause them to uncontrollably vomit when fed, offering little nutritional benefit, and raising the specter of lung infections and respiratory complications if they inhale their vomit. The feeding tube under these conditions may become disproportionate and unduly burdensome, and therefore non-obligatory.

> In some instances, providing drips and nasogastric feeding tubes can interfere with the natural course of dehydration in a way that causes acute discomfort to the patient facing imminent death. Intravenous fluids also tend to increase respiratory secretions, making it more difficult for patients to catch their breath or causing them to cough. Extra fluids may result in a need to suction the patient's lungs. Providing IV hydration can also cause a flare up of fluid accumulation in the abdomen and expand the edema layer around tumors, aggravating symptoms, particularly

pain. The use of IV drips and feeding tubes will always have to be evaluated in terms of the totality of the patient's condition, taking into account any undesirable effects, and the likelihood of benefit.

Notice how the pro-life position on assisted suicide is consistently against killing while not insisting on every possible means to keep someone alive. It accepts that there comes a point where one will raise the white flag of surrender to the thief called death. Some interventions, even care, might not be pursued. Having said that, in other cases, some interventions and care must be pursued.

Consider the story of Terri Schiavo. She was a young American woman who, in 1990, collapsed at home and went several minutes without oxygen. As a result, she acquired a brain injury. She eventually came out of a coma, but due to difficulty swallowing, she required a feeding tube. In this case, the feeding tube was not excessively burdensome for her body, and it was showing a hope of benefit: her body was capable of processing nutrients. Terri even showed some cognitive progress the following year when she was able to speak some words at rehabilitation sessions.

Her husband, Michael, had guardianship of Terri, but he got into a relationship with another woman and had children with her all while Terri was in care. Furthermore, when Terri developed a urinary tract infection (UTI), which is simply cured by antibiotics, Michael denied such treatment. A law overrode his wishes, but the fact that he wanted to stop proportionate treatment is alarming. Providing antibiotics in the presence of her UTI was not excessively burdensome, and it had a hope of benefit.

To make a long story short, a legal battle ensued for years, and ultimately Michael succeeded in having stopped what was, in Terri's case, proportionate care of nutrition and hydration. Terri's feeding tube was removed, and she was even denied hydration or nutrition by mouth. It took almost two weeks of her suffering before she succumbed to death by severe dehydration.

In this case, Terri did not have an underlying disease that was killing her. She didn't have, for example, end-stage stomach cancer that could make receiving food burdensome. Instead, she was a woman who developed a disability and required help receiving the care of food and water. She didn't die from a disease; she died by intentional killing, by way of severe dehydration.

HOW DOES THE PRINCIPLE OF DOUBLE EFFECT APPLY IN A PARTICULAR INTERVENTION?

Sometimes, when people commit an action, that act produces both good and bad effects. How does one determine whether the original course of action may be ethically pursued? This is where the principle of double effect is a helpful guide. The conditions of this principle are as follows:

1. The action in itself must be good or indifferent. The action must not be intrinsically evil.
2. The good effect cannot be obtained through the bad effect (because then the end would justify the means).
3. There must be a proportion between the good and bad effects brought about (e.g., life against life); the foreseen beneficial effects must be equal to or greater than the foreseen harmful effects (the proportionate judgment).

4. The intention of the subject must be directed toward the good effect while merely tolerating the bad effect.
5. Some say there is also a fifth requirement: that there does not exist another possibility or avenue.

We can consider these requirements in light of administering pain medication. What if doing so will have an effect of shortening a person's life? Would that be considered euthanasia / assisted suicide, or is it ethical?

The action of administering pain medication when someone is in pain is a good, not an evil, action, so it fulfills the first condition. From that good action may flow two effects: the good effect is the alleviation of pain; the bad effect may be the shortening of the patient's life. The pain is alleviated, not by way of the other effect of shortening a patient's life, but by way of the direct action of administering pain medications. There is proportion between these effects, and the intention is directed toward the good effect. Of course, if there were pain medication that only had the good effect and not the bad, then that ought to be used. But in the absence of an alternative, it is not killing a person to administer painkillers; it is killing pain.

It is worth noting that when administering painkillers, only the amount necessary to actually alleviate the pain should be administered. If someone gives more painkiller than necessary (wrong action) with the intention of hastening death (wrong intention), then that is immoral. But if someone gives the amount of painkiller necessary to alleviate pain (good action) with the intention of helping the patient (good intention), then that is moral.

It is also worth mentioning that although this example helps us understand the principle of double effect, it doesn't follow that administering pain medication will necessarily shorten one's life. In fact, a friend of mine who is a palliative care physician told me, "There is good evidence that proper pain control actually lengthens life while controlling pain." The point in all of this is to recognize that while death will come to us, we should not play the grim reaper and be the dealer of death. Instead, we ought to alleviate suffering without eliminating the sufferer.

Calvary Hospital in New York achieves this goal; it is America's "only hospital dedicated to providing hospice and palliative care to adult patients with advanced cancer and other life-limiting illness." The hospital's executive medical director emeritus is Dr. Michael J. Brescia, who transformed the world of medicine and ethics in two significant ways: 1) He coinvented the Brescia-Cimino arteriovenous fistula, which helped fifty thousand people in the first year and millions still today. 2) He prioritized people over profits by releasing his invention immediately instead of handing it over to a drug company, which would have delayed its release by a year (even though that patent would have made Dr. Brescia huge sums of money).

In an interview, he said the following: "At Calvary, we have never, ever, in any way, hastened death purposely. We'll argue, 'We love you enough to never kill.' We come across a symptom that is unacceptable, and we treat the symptom until there is relief. Our doctrine is succor, compassion, love, gentleness."

He also remarked, "At Calvary we treat 6,000 patients a year, and no one, after they have been here for 24 hours, asks for assisted suicide. No one: no matter what's wrong, and we've seen some terrible cases. Not when you reach out with arms of love."

5

Human Dignity Is Unconditional

The greatest disease in the West today is not TB or leprosy; it is
being unwanted, unloved, and uncared for. We can cure physical
diseases with medicine, but the only cure for loneliness, despair,
and hopelessness is love. There are many in the world who are
dying for a piece of bread but there are many more dying for a
little love.

—St. Teresa of Kolkata

It was Lent several years ago when a nineteen-year-old Canadian
teenager set off on a pilgrimage to the Holy Land—well, that's how
she described her plan to her friends. But where she was going was
not the traditional Holy Land of Israel where Christ once walked;
instead, her Holy Land would take her to India where Christ still
walked—in the suffering human souls she would serve. "We all
have the desire to help somebody, to do something good," said
Grace, one of my audience members, "but for me it was more that
I wanted to meet Christ and have an encounter with him, and I
knew that's what Mother Teresa and her sisters found in the poor."

It was the most solemn day of the Christian calendar—Good Friday, the day where followers of Christ around the world remember the sacrifice of Jesus laying down his life on the cross. For the volunteers at the Missionaries of Charity's home for the dying, this is a day off to enter into prayer and reflection. Grace, however, felt compelled to ask for a special exception: Since the sisters had to serve the sick that day anyway, could she help them as long as she did so slowly and in a spirit of prayer? They said yes, providing an opportunity for Grace to enter deeply into the Stations of the Cross in a way more real than ever before.

When one reads of Christ's Passion, we see how some close to him betrayed and abandoned him. But then there were the others—those like Simon of Cyrene and Mary his mother—who stood by his side and comforted him by their presence. This was the example Grace knew she ought to follow. At one point she found herself kneeling beside the bed of a dying man and slowly and patiently administrating hydration through a dropper; it was then that the words of Christ appeared in her mind: "I thirst" (John 19:28 NABRE). A crucifix on the wall reminded her of Christ dying on the cross, and she knew she was also encountering Christ in the individual lying in the bed before her. While incapable of eliminating suffering, she did what she could to alleviate it.

These moments taught that loving glances, hand-holding, and gentle patience can bring much peace to those who are suffering; even just sitting with them can be a consolation. As Grace remarked, "Regardless of what life experiences a person has had before death, when they go through such great suffering it has a transformative power; when the person allows himself to be loved and cared for by others, there's such a deep and beautiful reflection of God's love between the sufferer and the one who is suffering with."

Some people who arrived at Mother Teresa's home were extremely sick and expected to die, but with good care they were restored to health. Others, however, had their last breath—not on a dirty street ignored by passersby, but in a home surrounded by people caring for them. Grace told me that the few deaths she saw were incredibly peaceful: "I think it's because the patients knew they were loved."

She shared another story about a man who had a facial cancer. Most of his face was distorted or missing as a result: his jaw was gone, even some of his neck, so that it was just his eyes and the bridge of his nose; the rest was bandaged off. "I had the honor of being able to be with him the last half an hour before he died," Grace shared (although she didn't know at the time he was so close to death). "I remember making eye contact with him across the room for the first time and then going to see him and greet him, and that was the moment that bound my heart to Christ, and the dying, and the home for the dying." She didn't see the grotesqueness of what cancer had done to his face; instead, she told me that she peered deep into his eyes and was captivated by the beauty of his soul.

We acknowledge the dignity of a human being who is sick and fragile by treating him with reverence. Grace explained how this was upheld at the home for the dying: she and the others would assist men with shaving, brush women's hair, and help patients brush their teeth. The fact that the individuals were dying did not mean that such basic grooming should be withheld. Far from it; to do such simple acts was to stress the dignity of the person—to acknowledge that they were worth caring for regardless of their condition.

I've therefore been mystified by the notion of assisted suicide advocates that to be denied assisted suicide is to be denied a death with "dignity." The not-so-subtle implication is that if one dies naturally, entirely dependent on others to feed him, change him, or wipe his drool, that he has somehow lost his dignity.

Consider these words of a wife and mother named Liz, who was struck with advanced incurable kidney cancer: "The moment we label suicide an act of dignity, we've implied that people like me are undignified for not ending our lives; or worse, we're a costly burden for society. What a lonely, uncharitable, and fake world we live in if we think it's somehow undignified to let people see us suffer, to love us and care for us to the end."

A simple dictionary definition of dignity is this: "the quality or state of being worthy, honored, or esteemed." A sick person, a dying person, cannot lose her dignity because she *is*; in other words, by her very existence, she ought to be honored, respected, and cared for.

Consider that when something is valuable in and of itself, we act differently around it; we treat it as its nature demands. Consider an expensive, one-of-a-kind painting: a museum curator is going to make sure the valuable artwork is handled with care. Or consider a sleeping newborn baby: parents will walk quietly and gently into the bedroom to check on the child, avoiding making startling noises. When a painting is covered with dust or a baby soils her diaper, we do not say these have lost their dignity; rather, we respond in such a way as to acknowledge the dignity that lies within (by dusting the painting and changing the child).

So ought our response be to those who are dying: not hastening death, not eliminating the person, but instead being present and caring for the individual with the gentleness and reverence that their dignity inspires.

This perspective brings to mind a news story about a Parisian apartment being untouched for decades so that those who entered it seemed to walk back in time. In 2010, its owner, Mrs. De Florian, passed away, and the suite that she owned—but hadn't lived in for decades—became a goldmine discovery of countless valuable antiques. Because it appeared to have been unlived in for seventy years, the interior was covered in a thick layer of dust and cobwebs. Amidst it all was a painting by Italian artist Giovanni Boldini that was subsequently auctioned for 1.8 million euros. Here's the point: that piece of art was still considered valuable. It did not lose its value just because dust had settled on it. It did not lose its value just because it had not been admired for decades. It did not lose its value just because its existence had been unknown. Its worth was there all along, and discovering its existence was a reminder of that worth, one resulting in *restoration* and *appreciation*. So it is with humans: when a person's dignity is covered by "dust" or hidden and unknown, our response should be to restore and appreciate, not reject the other as having "lost" their dignity.

Think about the meaning of the word love. In Greek, there are at least four words to denote the different types of love: *agape, eros, philia,* and *storge*. *Agape* love indicates unconditional love. It is the most profound of all the loves because it involves knowing another's weaknesses, wounds, mistakes, sins, and brokenness and yet loving them in spite of it all. It is loving without conditions.

Human dignity, like *agape* love, should be viewed as similarly unconditional. Because humans are made in God's image (Gen. 1:27), because it was after God made humans that he surveyed his creation and described it as "very good" (Gen. 1:31) instead of the previously used word "good" that the rest of creation was described as, because God sent his only Son for the salvation of humans and not for other creatures (John 3:16), it follows that humans have dignity. Sin does not destroy our dignity; it defaces our dignity. Even the actions of a mass murderer do not cause him to lose his dignity. Instead, his actions cause him to mar, to soil, or to betray his dignity.

Think about what happens when someone is sick and dying. There is much that seems to be a betrayal of her dignity: vomiting, soiling herself, tumors, disfigurement, pain, fevers, and so forth. These things do not take away one's dignity, but they should prompt us to respond so as to affirm the dignity that is there but might seem as though it is covered up. Assisting someone's suicide does not affirm their dignity; it disregards it. It feeds into the false idea that their dignity was lost when their health and abilities were lost. Tenderly caring for someone and improving their circumstances is what reaffirms, time and again, that they have dignity.

That is what makes the story of Martin Pistorius both terribly tragic and incredibly beautiful. I think the best place to begin is where Martin does in his book *Ghost Boy: The Miraculous Escape of a Misdiagnosed Boy Trapped Inside His Own Body*. He starts by referencing Barney, the purple dinosaur. We are all likely familiar with the childlike jingle Barney sang. And let's be honest: it's rather annoying to hear, especially again and again. So imagine being subjected to that song day in and day out. For years. Imagine hating it, but not being able to tell the people subjecting you to it that that's how you feel. Imagine not being able to communicate your disdain because you cannot speak.

Now imagine sitting in a wheelchair and being strapped in because you have lost control of your body and might fall out. Now imagine the strap is digging into you and it hurts. But imagine you cannot tell anyone that's what is happening because, again, you cannot communicate. So you are forced to sit in agony.

Or imagine it's time for a shower and your caregiver splashes cold water on you and gets soap in your eyes, as though you do not feel the terrible sting. But you do. And it hurts.

These are just a few of the examples of suffering Martin faced while he endured ten years of being "locked in"—a functioning mind trapped in a barely functioning body. It all began in the 1980s when he was growing up in South Africa and became sick at the age of twelve. What appeared as the flu got progressively worse, so that Martin would sleep constantly and cease being able to talk. His muscles wasted and his limbs became spastic. His hands and feet curled in on themselves like claws. For the first few years of his illness he was not aware, but then something happened: Martin began to wake up. Except no one realized that. And for almost a decade, he was like a mind "trapped" in a body, in that he couldn't communicate as expected. The sufferings outlined above don't even come close to other agonies he would face, such as torturous physical and sexual abuse at the hands of some of his caregivers.

Because Martin could no longer do what he once did, because he was regressing rather than progressing, because he appeared to be unaware, some people treated him like trash. Their actions showed that they did not see unconditional dignity in him. Instead, dignity to them was *conditional*—and Martin simply did not reflect the right conditions.

From the perspective of unconditional dignity, however, it doesn't matter if Martin was aware or not; it doesn't matter if he would get unlocked (as he eventually did) or not. What mattered was that he existed and should have been reverenced because of that.

Someone who had that correct perspective and who was also mightily perceptive would come along and make a discovery. Her discovery was not of Martin's dignity, for she already recognized that; instead, her discovery was of Martin's unleashed potential.

Her name was Virna. And when I read about her in Martin's book, the beauty of her soul made me want to cry. Virna is the epitome of how we all should interact with another.

She was a caregiver who would use sweet-smelling essential oils to tenderly massage onto Martin's twisted body. She stood out because of her love.

Martin writes, "Virna looked at me properly. . . . She saw that my eyes really were the windows to my soul and became more and more convinced that I understood what she said. . . . Others wash and wipe, dress and dust me down, but it's always as a means to an end. Only Virna touches me for no other reason than to soothe my aching body."

Virna did not believe that Martin had the mind of a six-month-old baby as doctors had said. She thought that he should be sent for testing to see if he could communicate. She became an advocate for him, stressing to his parents how important it was to look into what his actual abilities were.

Thanks to Virna, Martin became unlocked. What has become of him today? He has regained the use of his upper body. He communicates via computer. He enters wheelchair races. He drives a car with his hands. He has given a TED talk. He got married. And in 2018, he and his wife had a baby boy.

How many people are alive today and mistreated like Martin once was? Rather than assisted suicide, we ought to affirm their dignity as Virna did Martin's. And we should remember that Virna treated Martin with tenderness *before* he got unlocked. Her kindness was not because of what he could become; it was because of who he *was*. Whether the sick and elderly in our midst "come out" of their lack of awareness or not, our job is to tenderly care for them. Our job is to be like Virna.

Just as people misunderstood Martin, some misunderstand God. In moments that are tough and painful, we can be tempted to get angry at God, wondering why he doesn't use his power in ways we would. Martin, however, trusted in God's loving presence and wisdom even when so much around him was confusing. Martin wrote, "The one person I talked to was God. . . . He was real to me, a presence inside and around that calmed and reassured me. . . . I talked to Him endlessly because I knew we shared something important. I didn't have proof that He existed, but I believed in Him anyway because I knew He was real. God did the same for me. Unlike people, He didn't need proof that I existed—He knew I did."

Having said that, what if some proponents of assisted suicide do not object to the main point of this chapter? What if they say they mean something different by "dignity" when they speak of "dying with dignity"? What if they mean someone should be able to "die without embarrassment," thus implying that reliance on others, particularly when one is very vulnerable and needing others for one's private care, is embarrassing? What if they aren't meaning to say that the person who rejects assisted suicide lacks dignity in her nature, but instead are meaning to say that the person who embraces assisted suicide wants dignity in the particular mode she uses to die?

Even with that perspective, there are problems. Going back to the aforementioned definition of dignity, one must ask: How does killing oneself lead to a state of being worthy, honored, or esteemed? Do we have a right not to be embarrassed? Even when we are embarrassed, does that give us license to do *just anything* to get out of the embarrassment? Do we really want to say embarrassment justifies killing? How does dying in weakness, pain, and reliance on others translate into a mode of death that lacks dignity? Simply put, it doesn't. In fact, it is moments of amplified weakness and fragility that draw compassion out of others and reinforce that we are worthy of their attention, that we are to be honored by their care, and that we are to be held in high regard by them.

6

Human Flourishing Occurs in a Context of Connection

Can an expired passport lead to dramatic, painful, and life-altering turns? That was the experience for one British teenager back in 2009.

When Henry Fraser was just seventeen years old, he scheduled a trip to go on vacation with some friends from school, traveling from his home of England to the beaches of Portugal. When he got in line to board the plane, an airline worker observed something Henry had not noticed: his passport was expired. While his friends continued their journey, Henry dejectedly returned home. His parents knew how much the trip meant to him and quickly put plans in motion to make it possible for Henry to achieve his dream. Little did any of them know that a seemingly simple and loving gesture would quickly turn a dream into a nightmare.

After a two-hundred-mile drive to a passport office, Henry found himself with an updated and expedited passport and on a new flight, landing in Portugal only twenty-four hours later than planned. After several days of fun in the sun, during a particularly hot moment on the beach, Henry ran into the ocean to cool off.

But a seemingly fun decision to dive into the water would lead to Henry's head colliding with the seabed, leaving him paralyzed from the shoulders down.

In Henry's memoir about his trauma and triumph, about his suffering and survival, he shares an inspiring insight about facing hardship. Although he would have to relearn how to breathe, cough, and swallow, although he would continue to live without being able to move his arms or legs as before, over a decade later Henry Fraser is not just surviving; he is thriving. What led to this human flourishing?

Although there are various factors, what is abundantly clear upon reading his book, *The Little Big Things: A Young Man's Belief that Every Day Can be a Good Day*, is the life-giving power of human connection. Henry's family stood by his side, enabling him to know, at the depths of his being, that he "wasn't alone." He wrote about his parents, who spent so much time in his presence, doing activities with him like crosswords, or reading to him, or simply updating him about the lives of their loved ones outside the hospital.

He also wrote, "With the love of others, whoever they are, you can face darkness and look through to the other side." When reflecting on his three brothers coming to his bedside, he said, "It was as if their tears and bear hugs were giving me a massive surge of life and I knew, in those moments, that with my brothers by my side, I would survive this."

If being carried by others can help a paralyzed person move forward, what makes someone become stagnant?

That question is answered in the movie *A Man Called Ove*, based off of the novel by Fredrik Backman. This Swedish film with English subtitles tells the tale of a grumpy old man with no desire to live. In fact, in his isolation and misery, Ove tries, repeatedly, to kill himself. As it happens, each time he comes close to succeeding, an unsuspecting neighbor calls on him for help. As the film progresses, the viewer begins to understand why Ove is as he is. The unfolding backstory reveals what is under the surface. This allows one to see Ove with new eyes—to see his goodness and his pain and therefore to empathize with him. As the heartwarming film unfolds, these key themes emerge: 1) Isolation and disconnection lead to despair. Ove is miserable not just because he has experienced profound suffering. (After all, his neighbors also experience suffering but do not share his same misery.) Ove is miserable because he is isolated. 2) Relationship can unlock the door to a person's heart. 3) When a person is *needed by* others, it teaches him that he *needs* others. (The reverse is also true.)

Humans are made for relationship. How do we know this? First, we can look to the first creation story, when God said, "Let us make humankind in our image, according to our likeness" (Gen. 1:26). God is a Trinity, three persons in one. God is a communion of the Father, Son, and Holy Spirit, who are in a relationship of continually giving and receiving love. Humans, then, image God by being in a relationship of giving and receiving love.

We can see this in the power humans have to create new life. The very beginning of the next generation is designed to come through a communion of persons. Whereas the circulatory system, respiratory system, or endocrine system is complete in an individual, the reproductive system is incomplete. Each individual has only half of that system. For it to work at its fullness, one needs the other half, which comes from another person. By God's designs, to *create* another human is to first *cleave* to another human, to create a communion of persons. Then, once new life is created, that life is nestled beneath the heart of the mother. Once again, we do not have life in isolation; we have a new person who, by very design, needs another and is in communion with another. Love and life necessitate connection.

In the second creation story, when God creates the world, God looks at Adam and, amid all the beauty of his creation, remarks, "It is not good that the man should be alone" (Gen. 2:18). It doesn't take much to see what happens when man is alone. We need only look to solitary confinement as a torture technique to see what happens when humans are removed from a communion of persons.

In the movie *Walk the Line*, based on the true story of musician Johnny Cash, there is a poignant scene where the characters of Johnny Cash and his first wife, Vivian Liberto, are fighting. The beginning of their marriage had involved poverty and work challenges, but as Johnny rose to fame, he also rose in wealth. That wealth, however, came with a price: he was often away. As the two have a battle of words, Johnny looks at pregnant Vivian and lists all the things he got for her: a dream house, pretty things, and a car. He then demands, "What do you want from me?" Her answer? "I want you, John! I want you!"

Where relationships are broken, humans experience profound suffering. Why? Because we are made for relationship—not things. And things are made for us—not the other way around.

Consider filmmaker Roko Belic, who once asked, "Why is it that people who have so little and have suffered so much seem to be happier than other people who are more fortunate?" He presents the answer in his 2011 documentary *Happy*. While there are various factors that contribute to our happiness, such as enjoying the beauty of nature, a key factor is satisfying relationships. The film shows that regardless of living with poverty, old age, or a disfigurement from a traumatic accident, we experience happiness when we have people to commune with.

Tal Ben-Shahar reinforced this point in 2019 at La Ciudad de las Ideas (CDI), an event similar to Ted Talks that I was speaking at in Puebla, Mexico. Shahar is a professor who teaches the most popular course at Harvard on positive psychology, which is all about happiness. He was a fellow presenter at the event and emphasized that relationships with people, rather than things, is a determining factor in happiness. He talked about a psychology experiment where people were given money and told to buy themselves something; following that, their mood and happiness were measured. Similarly, people were given money and told to donate it to someone or some cause; subsequently, that group's happiness was also measured. The latter group showed longer-lasting happiness than the former. He then used that point to reference something from his first language, which is Hebrew. He said that his favorite name is "Natan," which is a palindrome that is spelled the same forward and backward. The name means "to give," and his message was that when you give, you receive.

But, in order to give, you need someone to give to; you need relationship. When children go to school, we often think about what adults can teach them. And yet, unknowingly, it is children that have the most profound lesson of all to teach adults: we need each other. Think about the utter vulnerability of a newborn baby who relies on someone to do everything for her. Consider five-year-olds who, if left to their own devices, would probably eat cereal for every meal.

The need for children (and thus adults) to have strong relationships has led to a fascinating body of research related to attachment theory. In a book about the attachment styles of secure attachment, anxious attachment, and avoidant attachment, authors Amir Levine and Rachel Heller write about the importance of healthy, close, loving relationships. When writing about the pitfalls of the avoidant attachment style, they reference the book *Into the Wild*. They talk about its main character, Chris, who sought to live self-reliantly. In his trek to the Alaskan wilderness, he met people who wanted him to be a part of their lives, but he rejected that. In his rugged individualism, he lived for months on his own until he died. Shortly before his passing, he wrote in his journal, "Happiness [is] only real when shared."

What Chris learned the hard way is what children, by their very existence, teach us: we need relationship. And as the "circle of life" does a 360, we typically end as we began: teaching the "doers" around us that we are made to "be" in relationship. The elderly, the frail, the sick—they, like children, become the next teachers of one of life's great lessons: "Be. Be with me. Be connected. And as I am who I am in all my vulnerability—in my need—that will unleash from you great love." In needing to be loved, the beloved teaches a lesson to the lover: not only is there joy in loving, but the lover needs to be loved in return. Only in relationship can we experience life's greatest lesson. But assisted suicide robs us of that because it eliminates the very person to be in relationship with.

In June 2018, *Maclean's Magazine* published an article titled "Canada's Loneliest People" with a troubling subtitle: "25 per cent of Canadian seniors live alone, but there lies a little-documented population within that demographic that live in acute isolation."

The article reports on people going weeks without connection with others, and in desperation calling 911.

The article discusses what are termed "elder orphans." It describes the fate of some older people living in populated areas who, due to their fragility, cannot leave their homes. They end up being completely isolated, and even when food is brought to them through meal delivery programs, it is dropped off for them to eat alone.

The article goes on: "One patient, who still has children and no serious medical concerns, asked . . . about medically assisted dying—'not actively suicidal but feels she doesn't have pleasure in her life anymore.'"

Two years later, COVID restrictions would make isolation and loneliness worse. In 2020, CTV News reported about a ninety-year-old woman who received assisted suicide in Canada. She had enjoyed her life: she was social, active, and got out. But then COVID restrictions hit. As the news reported, these "ended her daily walks, library visits and all the activities in her Toronto retirement home. Her daughter says they had plastic dividers in the dining rooms and supervised visits in the garden. 'She, almost overnight, went from a very active lifestyle to a very limited life, and they had, very early on, a complete two week confinement just to her room,' Tory [her daughter] said." The woman suffered a decline as a result.

When the winter of 2020 approached, she feared similar isolation and restrictions would make her life miserable. Her first request for assisted suicide was denied. Her daughter said when she applied a second time she had "more concrete medical health" issues and she was granted assisted suicide. The news was quick to report that the woman had, pre-COVID, planned on making use of Canada's assisted suicide laws down the road. But the impact of COVID restrictions certainly sped up her timeline. As the daughter pointed out, "She just truly did not believe that she wanted to try another one of those two-week confinements into her room."

These stories should cause us to pause and deeply consider the solution. People who are disconnected, isolated, and lonely are suffering. The solution, rather than introducing assisted suicide, is to introduce a better environment for a lonely person—an environment of relationship and connection—so that we eliminate the adjective "lonely" rather than the noun "person."

It is worth considering that throughout the Scriptures there are many references to God's concern for orphans and widows and his command that we share his concern:

- "In you the orphan finds mercy." (Hosea 14:3)
- "Religion that is pure and undefiled before God, the Father, is this: to care for orphans and widows in their distress." (James 1:27)
- "Learn to do good; seek justice, rescue the oppressed, defend the orphan, plead for the widow." (Isa. 1:17)
- "Give justice to the weak and the orphan; maintain the right of the lowly and the destitute." (Ps. 82:3)
- "The LORD . . . upholds the orphan and the widow." (Ps. 146:9)
- "I will not leave you orphaned." (John 14:18)
- "For the LORD your God . . . executes justice for the orphan and the widow." (Deut. 10:17–18)
- "You shall not wrong any widow or orphan." (Exod. 22:21 NABRE)

Although it may seem obvious, it is important to ask the question "*Why* are we commanded to care for, and not harm, orphans and widows? *Why* are they mentioned in particular? *Why* would God set them apart?" I think the answer lies in their neediness. Orphans and widows are disconnected from what (who, really) they need. Children wouldn't survive without people caring for them. In ancient times, women would not survive without the support and provision of husbands or families. Orphans and widows are individuals whose very ability to live is in jeopardy.

But the issue is more than material means. When one thinks of orphans and widows, what comes to mind is "aloneness" and "loneliness." Rather than ignore, abandon, or eliminate them, we are called to uphold, give justice to, care, rescue, and defend them. And all of those duties involve connection; they involve being in relationship. This is not only true for the lonely souls of biblical times; it is just as true for people of today who may be sick, elderly, or terminally ill. We are commanded to love and serve them too.

7

We Ought to Celebrate Being

When two people meet for the first time, almost immediately a common question is asked: "What do you do?" It's interesting how we humans gravitate toward our activity as the topic of conversation. Perhaps it's because we are capable of so much and do so many varied things. While our actions can be impressive, what if they aren't?

I remember many years ago seeing a billboard advertisement by the Canadian Down Syndrome Society. It showed a picture of a little girl with Trisomy 21 alongside the caption "Celebrate Being." I loved it! In a world that celebrates "doing," that celebrates accomplishment, worldly success, etc., we must not forget that there would be no doing if there were not first a human being. Even if a human being cannot "do" in the present moment, if he still "is," he should be celebrated. The danger that arises when we celebrate doing more than being is that our very identity can get caught up in our accomplishments, so that when we can no longer do, we think we should no longer be.

That brings to mind the story of Dr. David Goodall. He had accomplished much in his long life, living to the age of 104. He was a scientist in ecology and botany, teaching at universities in several countries. He was a researcher and editor and outside of his profession enjoyed acting, performing on stage for decades. He even played tennis until he was ninety years old. He had married three times and had both children and grandchildren. But his death in 2018 was not due to illness; rather, it was due to his own hand. He traveled from Australia to Switzerland, where he was killed by assisted suicide.

As I researched his story, these details stood out to me:

- One of his daughters said, "He wasn't a very good husband. He was a very, very difficult man because he was so focused on the science." She said her dad had never said "I love you" and only did so when she drew it out of him the day he committed assisted suicide.
- Two years before the assisted suicide, the university where he worked as an honorary research associate considered him unfit to work on campus (even though it was an unpaid position). He challenged this and won but was given an alternative workspace.
- The year after that, he fell at home and was helpless on the floor for two days before his cleaner found him.
- His eyesight was declining, and he had long given up his driver's license.
- In an interview he said, "At my age, I get up in the morning. I eat breakfast. And then I just sit until lunchtime. Then I have a bit of lunch and just sit. What's the use of that?" He also said, "*I am not happy. I want to die.*"

- A week preceding the assisted suicide he visited family in France and "was full of life," the observing reporter said. While there, David was surrounded by the beauty of the countryside and was with family. Asked what he liked about this place he had visited so often, he remarked, "Well, it's mainly the people here."

Dr. Goodall was undoubtedly experiencing much loss. And the pain of that shouldn't be minimized. The thought of him lying weak and alone on the floor for days is utterly terrible. Why did embracing death have to be the solution to his suffering? How is that the best we can do? What if, instead of assisted suicide, he no longer lived alone? What if there were more to his days than sitting between meals? What if that space was filled with companionship? What if university students signed up to visit him, listening to the wisdom he had to impart and sharing their experiences and lives with him? What if he spent more time in France with the family and animals and countryside that were so uplifting for him? What if, after a lifetime of "doing," his ongoing living was to learn—and teach others—the power of "being"?

In Washington State there is an award-winning Intergenerational Learning Center that blends childcare under the same roof as a living facility for elders. From infancy to five years old, young children are in an environment with older adults, brought together to interact with each other. Whether the means for connection is activities, music, or dance, at the heart of it all is celebrating being. It is about being connected, being in relationship, being in the present moment, and it becomes life-giving to both parties.

In a PBS story about the program, Charlene Boyd, the administrator of Providence Mount St. Vincent (the living center for elders), said, "All of us have common needs to be recognized. All of us have common needs to be loved, and all of us have common needs to share life together."

Being recognized. Loved. Sharing life with others. That is what Dr. Goodall *needed*. He understandably *wanted* to drive, *wanted* to act, *wanted* to see better, *wanted* to do all kinds of things his frail body could no longer do. But in reality, he didn't need those things. His needs, however, were legitimate; they were necessary for human flourishing: recognition, love, and connection.

How can we be more intentional about meeting people's legitimate needs? My friend Kathleen comes to mind. She shared this experience from when she lived in Western Canada:

> Every Friday morning, I've been spending an hour playing *Scrabble* with a lovely ninety-three-year-old lady at a local care home. It's my simple way of helping the elderly find joy in their daily life. I'm always praying for opportunities to talk to her about God, or to simply show her that she is loved. Today, that opportunity came in full force.
>
> After our game, she outright asked me, "What do you think of doctor-assisted suicide?" and pointed to an article from the paper on the topic. I told her that I felt it was very sad that anyone should feel the need to take their life, and it's our failure as a society when anyone is left feeling this way. After some time discussing this, she expressed to me that she can sympathize with people who don't feel they have a reason to live in their suffering, as she, too, often wonders why God still has her "stuck in this wheelchair."

With tears in my eyes, I was able to tell her what a joy she is to me, and that I look forward to visiting her every week. She teared up as well, shock in her eyes, and said, "Really? Is that true?" I nodded, unable to get more words out. "Well then, perhaps there is reason enough for me to be here."

Or take another friend of mine, a nursing student. She saw on a patient's chart that the patient had made an inquiry about euthanasia. My friend intentionally visited that patient more than others. Rather than discuss euthanasia, she spent time getting to know the woman. She became interested in her life; she connected over common interests and common backgrounds; she smiled and was joyful; she engaged the patient in conversation. In short, she poured love out on her. A few weeks later, when my friend checked the patient's record, there was a note indicating the patient was no longer interested in euthanasia.

Connection holds great power, as my friends' stories prove, and intergenerational interactions can reinforce this. I recall the insights I had when my family gathered to celebrate my mom's seventy-fifth birthday. I sat at the table cuddling the latest addition to our family: my three-month-old nephew Carl. As I cradled Carl, I felt the increasing temperature of the blanket on my lap that swaddled his body: "Did he pee through his diaper?" I wondered. "Or is that just warmth from body heat?" Thankfully, it was the latter, but it caused me to reflect on the total dependency of Carl on other people. And then my mind wandered to the elderly, some of whom are just as dependent on others as babies are. And with society's increasing acceptance of euthanasia, a thought came to me: "What if the world treated Carl like it sometimes treats the elderly?"

Would we leave him in his crib alone all day, keeping the TV on for distraction but otherwise having minimal interaction with him? Would we scurry about to do lots of things but never take time simply to be with him? Would we consider ending his life because he can't do much, asking, "What's the point anyways?"

Now, some might say that Carl, as opposed to an individual at the end of her life, will one day be a "contributing" member to society, and his is a life we shouldn't end. In other words, we would preserve Carl's life for what might be, but we would end an old person's life for what is no more. But what if Carl never matured enough to do what most adults do? What if we knew he would only live for the next six months? Knowing that, would we kill him, or would we savor and celebrate the little time we have left?

And so, as I thought further, it occurred to me that our world would be a better place if we asked a different question: "What if we treated the elderly the way we treat Carl?"

If that were the case, we would sing and play music. We would smile, laugh, and engage. We would soothe during seasons of sadness. We would hug. We would look at the other and simply delight in them.

As I have watched my four other nieces and nephews interact with their littlest brother, I've noticed something: when vulnerable, needy people are in our midst, it can bring out our softer, gentler, more caring side.

I think about Carl's strong-willed older brother, who demonstrated such reverence for Carl, delighting in holding him and sweetly kissing his cheeks. I think about my other nephew, a very sensitive child, who held his crying baby brother and repeatedly said "Shh-shh-shh" until he had shh-ed him to sleep just like he had seen

WE OUGHT TO CELEBRATE BEING

his mom do. I think of my niece, who loves to sing, dance, and be loud but who, when I arrived one day, crawled out from under the kitchen table and said "Boo" in the quietest of whispers because Carl was nearby sleeping. I think of my then-nine-year-old niece, who is like a second mother to Carl and so good at comforting him, carrying her baby brother around like a doll.

Far from being a burden, the presence of Carl draws virtue out of the whole family. His need becomes an opportunity for our kindness. The same is true of the elderly—if only we let that be the case.

Many years ago, my sister texted me a story from her evening: She was trying to put her then-youngest baby, my niece Cecilia, to sleep and promised her oldest daughter, Monica, that she would come to her room later and read to her. But it took so long to put Cecilia down that by the time she got to Monica's room my eldest niece had fallen asleep—with the unread book in her limp hand. My sister texted me a photo explaining what happened with the caption "MOM GUILT!" So I texted back, "You've given Monica something better than a bedtime story—you've given her a sister." She excitedly responded, "RIGHT! Perspective! Perspective! It's all about perspective!"

I realize not everyone can give their child a sibling, but everyone can give their child, and themselves, encounters with others, be it the elderly or someone else. That doesn't mean such encounters are always easy in the moment; after all, consider the stories from chapter 1 of people who faced great suffering and challenges. The point here is that perspective is a powerful ally, and it is perspective that teaches us that encounters with the other can become moments to celebrate being in the human experience of love.

What are some specifics on how to celebrate being and thus make life richer? In our world filled with noise, sitting in silence can be like water to cracked soil. When we are quiet, we can more readily hear the still, small voice of God (1 Kings 19:12).

In the book *The Power of Silence: Against the Dictatorship of Noise*, Robert Cardinal Sarah says, "Silence is difficult, but it enables man to let himself be led by God. From silence is born silence. Through God the silent, we can gain access to silence. And man is unceasingly surprised by the light that pours forth then. . . . Silence is a quest and a form of charity, in which God's eyes become our eyes and God's heart is grafted onto our heart."

Besides sacred silence, there are other ways we can celebrate being. Have you ever just sat with another person, held their hand, closed your eyes, and experienced the closeness of their presence? Or have you done nothing except listen to a beautiful symphony with someone you care about? What about remembering being a child and having a story read to you? Or reading a story to a child? Or have you ever parked your car and watched the sun set over mountains or the ocean, and shared in that experience with another? Have you sat for a really long time at the beach, toes curled into the sand, feeling the descent of dusk lifting your spirits and triggering deep conversation? Have you found a sunny spot and let the heat of the sun warm your face, delighting in the simplicity of the experience?

Have you been around people who are laughing and begun laughing too? Have you watched children perform a goofy play or a song that they made up and observed how they are immersed in delight? Have you held in your arms a sleeping newborn baby and been captivated and content just to stare at him like you would at a fireplace in winter? Have you sat and simply smelled freshly baked cookies and then savored the taste with the baker?

I remember meeting a couple who told me that their relative would often bake cookies at midnight when her older children came home from being out with friends. She knew the delightful smell would entice them to the kitchen, providing an opportunity for a fruitful encounter with her children. It was so positive in maintaining a good relationship that she expanded her approach to a street outreach program, getting a storefront and baking cookies when young people came out of bars. This provided an alcohol-free environment with intentional opportunities for being in relationship with young people who often didn't have families to go home to.

These are the kinds of powerful moments of being that we can create for others and share in with them.

8

Some of the Best Things in Life Come When We Release Control

At a presentation I gave on assisted suicide, an audience member raised her hand and shared that a few months prior, her aunt had opted for assisted suicide. She shared that the aunt had been surrounded by her family and was well loved. She described the orchestrated death as "beautiful." She said her aunt had methodically gone through a bucket list, had fulfilled all of her dreams, and was full and satisfied by the life she had lived. She was even leaving a significant financial legacy to help with cancer research. In the aunt's mind, her life was done, so she opted for suicide assistance.

I asked the woman if she felt comfortable sharing more about her aunt's situation and condition. Since she was, the conversation continued in front of the crowd. I asked her what the aunt was dying from and what her health status was like before the assisted suicide. The woman shared that her aunt had cancer that had metastasized (spread to other parts of her body). She had a very bad heart. The more the woman described, the more it sounded to me like the patient would have been very near natural death. So I asked her if assisted suicide hadn't happened, how close to death she thought her aunt was—possibly weeks or even days? The woman, who had a medical background, indicated it probably would have been mere days. So I asked, "Then why do assisted suicide? If she was literally days away from death anyways, why not give her comfort and surround her with family and friends until she passed naturally?"

The audience member didn't have much of a response other than to indicate it was what the patient wanted. Situations like this reveal a serious challenge we are up against: desire for total control.

In 2014, the movie *The Giver* was released, which is based on Lois Lowry's book of the same name. It is a profoundly insightful dystopian story about a community that is built around "sameness." In this futuristic world, people no longer know loss, death, hatred, or violence. But the trade-off? They also no longer know love, empathy, compassion, and joy. They are numbed by daily injections that rob them of emotions, the depths of the human experience. They wear clothes, but there is no fashion. They have dwellings, but not homes. They can see, but only in gray rather than color. In effect, they are like robots. In the quest to avoid suffering, they have also avoided truly living. If they were able to feel deep affection and connection to another, then they would correspondingly feel the pain that comes when such a connection is severed. And so, every single aspect of society is meticulously controlled in order to avoid suffering.

It is perhaps an extreme example, but it nonetheless demonstrates how control can go too far. Our society, particularly North America, is obsessed with control. (And I can perhaps recognize this so readily because I am someone who struggles with her own inordinate desire for control at times.) But as *The Giver* reveals, trying to control everything comes with a cost. Are we willing to pay the price?

Consider the story shared by a nurse who works in palliative care. She told of a patient of hers who had "medical assistance in dying" (MAID). The patient had terminal metastatic breast cancer and did not want to continue living. Instead, she wanted a planned death that she could control and orchestrate. So she scheduled the date and time, selected music, and invited family members. The nurse explained how the patient had even gone so far as to sign a document outlining that "if for whatever reason she was no longer judged to be of sound mind at the time of the MAID provision, she could be euthanized anyways." But then something unexpected happened: the patient had a grand mal seizure. She was given medicine in response, but that left her, as the nurse described, "confused and groggy." What day did this grand mal seizure occur on? The day of her scheduled euthanasia. As the nurse described it, the patient was "unable to properly confirm she wanted the euthanasia, or say goodbye to her family members. She tried to speak but no one could understand what she was saying."

Life circumstances are unpredictable; time, however, is very predictable. The clock struck 6:00 p.m. Only hours had passed since the unexpected seizure. It was *the* time. With her attempts at speaking incoherent to those in the room, euthanasia was administered. The patient is dead, so we will never know what she was trying to communicate in her final moments. It is possible she had changed her mind. It is possible she wanted more time, given the sudden change of circumstances. Ironically, and sadly, in the end, this patient was not in control of a situation she had tried so desperately to control.

An audience member at a talk I gave once remarked that if someone only has a few days left, his approach would be to use the limited time to justify assisted suicide, rather than follow my approach of using that time to justify hanging on. *Nothing's going to happen in the days left*, he surmised, *so what's the point?*

First, as we saw earlier in the book, if we allow assisted suicide for the reason of closeness to death, it becomes entirely arbitrary. How does one determine what is justifiable "closeness"?

Second, the legacy such an individual leaves behind for loved ones (and anyone who knows about the suicide assistance) is that when a person decides they've had enough, it is perfectly acceptable to end it all. Is that really the message we want to teach the next generation, which is increasingly facing a suicide epidemic?

Most fundamentally, we simply cannot *know* that "nothing" is going to happen in the days left. We do not know how those days will unfold. We humans are not omnipotent; we are not fortune tellers. We can plan and control as much as we want, but we absolutely do not know exactly what the future holds—even if that future is short.

Consider a five-year-plan: people are encouraged to identify goals to aspire toward, but planning only gets us so far. How often have people looked *back* on a five-year-plan and observed how differently it unfolded than expected? Moreover, when we plan and control too much, we may create a future that is not as good as one built on surrender. (Consider that there's a reason the word "freak" is often attached to the word "control," and a reason why a therapist will highlight the pitfalls of inordinate control in relationships).

When we are obsessed with control, we act as though we know best and as though what we have planned is exactly how things should be.

How many times have we been *wrong*?

How many times have we been *surprised*?

How many times have we been *grateful* that things did not work out as we expected or even wanted?

What if another patient was to be impacted by the patient near death? What if long-suffering endurance, peaceful surrender, and loving community were to be lessons demonstrated to health care workers? What if the dying person was to have an epiphany about some regret in their past that they had been completely blind to? What if a patient in a semi-conscious state who couldn't communicate was, by their need and utter vulnerability, going to teach the people around them the merits of *being*, of loving, and of tenderness? What if this would only happen over the time period of natural death, and these would be missed opportunities if some form of suicide assistance or euthanasia were chosen? The possibilities are endless, but the point is this: the possibilities exist, if we allow them to.

So what if, when death comes knocking, we didn't answer? What if this wasn't denial or running away but simple acceptance? What if letting go of control meant letting death open the door itself without knowing the moment precisely? What if this almost unbearable waiting was for us to learn—at our end—what was man's downfall "in the beginning"—namely, that we humans are not in control, but God is? What if waiting for death to open the door was to teach us not to be afraid of letting go of control? What if it was to teach us that being led by an omnipotent source is better than trying to lead ourselves when we just do not see the full picture? What if it was to give us a newfound freedom we didn't think possible with our limited perspective?

Some might object and say there is no God; they may claim there is no higher power to surrender to. Although it is true that they believe there is no higher power to surrender to, it does not follow there *is* no god in such a person's world. On the contrary, the person who doesn't surrender to a higher power *does* have a god in their life: that god is themselves, insofar as it is they themselves that they hold as the final authority. But what if the self is a bad god? Since we know, without a doubt, that the self is prone to mistakes, errors, and vices and has limited knowledge, isn't it risky to put one's trust on such shaky ground?

Consider the following: Anyone who has purchased IKEA furniture knows all about assembling it. The manufacturer provides a simple image of how to put together the various parts. If you follow the instructions, you'll get a Poang chair to sit on or a bookshelf for your literature collection. Do we take offense that IKEA's designers tell the buyer what to do? Of course not, because IKEA has the buyer's best interests in mind; it wants happy customers who return. IKEA created the furniture and knows how it will most aesthetically, functionally, and safely live up to its designs. IKEA's "rules for assembly" are not meant to unfairly restrict us, deny us, or control us. They are meant to free us.

So it is with surrendering our control into the hands of an all-powerful God—a God who loved us so much that he lowered himself, entered into the human experience, and then suffered and was killed in our place so we could spend eternity with him in the ecstasy of heaven.

Of course, God gave us freedom to make decisions, but there is a significant difference between what we *can* do and what we *ought* to do. We *can* do anything, but we *ought* to do the right thing, that which was designed for our good. In big decisions and small, what is the thing we ought to do? That takes discernment. Even with surrender, we still have to make decisions (like the guidelines given in chapter 4 on proportionate versus disproportionate actions). Therefore, I would suggest there is a balancing act with control: taking action, even directing how you think things should be, while having a flexibility to work with things as they arise. It's about rejecting rigidity. It's about seeing the merits of applying some control without becoming a control freak.

Let me give an example of this dance I am proposing. Have you ever written down your dreams? If so, have you then, years later, read old journals and discovered what you once envisioned actually came to fruition? I have, and each time I had these experiences (there have been several), I was in awe of how what I hoped for came to be.

But here's the thing: in some cases, I had even forgotten I had had the dream, let alone written it down. So although in some ways I had made choices that influenced certain outcomes, there were so many factors I wasn't in control of that nonetheless occurred, unfolded, and contributed to the fulfilment of desire. Had I clung too tightly, had I tried too hard, had I been fixated on my timeline, with my limited knowledge, perhaps the dreams would not have unfolded. So there must be some give and take between acting and simply receiving, between directing and allowing for unfolding. It's like a dance: there's push and pull, give and take, leading and following.

In a sense, dying naturally is a similar balance: it embraces life, but it accepts that death will come; it tries different interventions, but it eventually accepts their futility; it doesn't run to death, but it acknowledges when death is approaching. And it is in that space between living and dying, in that waiting, where there is room for the unfolding of things in a way we could not know, imagine, or orchestrate. Assisted suicide, like other acts of total control and manipulation, rob the individual and society of the greatness, and the gift, of the unknown.

This dance of the push and pull of control reminds me of two people who both suffered brutally but differently: Brittany Maynard and Mattie Stepanek. The former's example is not to be followed, whereas the latter's is.

Brittany died by suicide assistance at the age of twenty-nine. She had terminal brain cancer and wanted to end her life *before* the predicted end-stage consequences of this terrible malady would come to fruition. When she did pass away, she wrote in advance on Facebook, "Today is the day *I have chosen* to pass away."

The interview with Brittany's husband, Dan, on the *Megyn Kelly TODAY* show is certainly heartbreaking. What Brittany had endured, and what she feared would only get worse, are terrible realities for anyone to face. Her husband framed things this way: if she hadn't chosen her controlled "gentle" death, she would have been "struggling and in pain." He said that her situation was already such that morphine wasn't adequately eliminating her pain. She faced brutal insomnia. There was nausea and vomiting. And as bad as that was, there were the seizures. He said that with grand mal seizures, she would bleed out of her mouth because she'd bite through her tongue. She feared blindness and paralysis, which were likely what would come with the growing tumor. That's not what Brittany wanted the experience of death to be like. Understandably —*no one* would want that.

Opponents of what she chose are not saying that if her death were that way, it would have been a pleasant thing. They would believe in working valiantly to alleviate the suffering of someone like Brittany. There are several strategies for pain control besides the morphine her husband said wasn't sufficient. These include more potent opioids, opioid adjuncts, nerve blocks, and so forth. Palliative care as a discipline has evolved markedly since its early days, and as a physician I know told me, practitioners can control pain in over 95 percent of cases. Inevitably, some will respond by asking, "What about the other five percent?" Not all suffering can be entirely eliminated; opponents of suicide assistance are making the simple but hard-to-accept point that ending your own life should not be the solution, no matter how terrible the circumstances. It is worth acknowledging, though, that pain can be managed in a majority of cases—and that is something that is often not realized and that leads many to live in fear of unmanaged pain.

When we release control, even when control is a means to avoid that which we fear, unexpected—even amazing—things can happen. And Mattie Stepanek is proof of that.

Mattie graced our earth for thirteen short years, but his rich, supernatural legacy is far more than most leave in a long lifetime.

Mattie's beginnings were almost his end. He was diagnosed with an extremely rare form of muscular dystrophy called dysauto-nomic mitochondrial myopathy, and it was predicted he would live for only hours after birth. But he defied the odds by living for more than a decade. His three older siblings, Katie, Stevie, and Jamie, had shorter fates, dying at the ages of twenty months, six months, and almost four years old respectively; they were also burdened by this brutal disease—but that wasn't discovered until after Mattie's birth. When a label was finally given for what the children had, the doctors uncovered that, unknowingly, their mother, Jeni, had been the genetic carrier of the condition, and that she herself would be invaded by an adult-onset version of it. Mattie and his mother not only suffered the loss of three siblings/children; they lived through seasons of profound poverty, relying on handouts. Little can be found online about Mattie's dad, but in an interview where Mattie was asked about him, the little boy simply said, "We're divorced from my father because he did some mean and scary things to us, and I don't like to point fingers or talk about him." When the interviewer said, "You don't see him?" Mattie simply said, "No."

Hospital stays and pain were a normal part of Mattie's life. He used a ventilator and a wheelchair, which is now his mother's fate. It gets worse: she was also diagnosed with cancer after Mattie died. If there were to be a case study in profound suffering, the Stepaneks would be a prime example. And yet, what they're known and admired for is mind-blowing resilience, otherworldly wisdom, and interminable hope.

When I first learned about this precious boy while writing this book, I was so inspired that I became hungry to discover as much as I could about him. Watching interviews of him left me wondering, "Was he even human? How could a young child speak such profound insights? Did an angel take on bodily form and present as Mattie Stepanek?" I recommend watching the full-length interview of him on *Larry King Live* at the age of eleven to see why I would ask these questions.

Starting at age three, Mattie began composing poetry, which his mother transcribed until he could write himself. He eventually published seven books. Millions came to know and love Mattie Stepanek. But here's the key: Mattie and his divinely inspired insights only became known throughout the world *after* he was on the brink of death. In 2001, when Mattie was on the cusp of turning eleven, doctors were convinced he was weeks or even days away from dying. He had slipped into several comas and was bleeding out of his fingers, his lips, his trachea, and his feet.

Mattie wanted to go home, but the doctors did not want that because they said that dying there would not enable them to provide pain management like they could if he stayed at the hospital. They were concerned that if he went home, his death would be agony.

It is that type of death many fear. It is that type of death some would want to avoid by way of assisted suicide. It is that type of death that, when it seems to be rapidly approaching, would make some declare, "What is the *point* of carrying on? What good could possibly happen? Let me just take control and make death happen now."

But what happened is that Mattie Stepanek prayed. What happened is that the bleeding stopped. What happened is that a miracle occurred. What happened is that the last three *years* of Mattie's life were just about to begin. What happened is that during that time period, his poetry, which he named *Heartsongs*, would be published. What happened is that his books would become *New York Times* bestsellers. What happened is that he would befriend former US president Jimmy Carter and appear on Oprah Winfrey's show several times, befriending her as well. What happened is that the world would come to know this tiny, fragile little sage named

Mattie Stepanek because, as he said to his mother, "I have to live until the moment I die."

We must never assume we know the future. We must never assume it's always best when we take control. Sometimes the most incredible things unfold when we release our grasping fingers and surrender to what may be.

When Mattie eventually did succumb to his illness, Jimmy Carter gave the eulogy at his funeral, saying, "We have known kings and queens, and we've known presidents and prime ministers, but the most extraordinary person whom I have ever known in my life is Mattie Stepanek."

Oprah mentioned the thousands upon thousands of shows she's done, interviewing so many people, and she said, "Mattie would be the single biggest relationship that ever developed out of a show." She described him as "one of the sweetest souls I have ever known."

And of her son, Jeni Stepanek said, "He seemed to know God rather than learn about God. God was always his friend. God walked with him. One of the most profound things he said to me . . . as he got closer to death and he knew he was dying even before I could accept that, he said, 'Even the silence of God gives me strength.'"

In an interview with Raymond Arroyo (who founded a guild with a mission to advance Mattie's possible cause of canonization), Jeni recounts a story of Mattie hearing a nearby baby crying while Mattie himself was dying in the ICU:

It's within a week of his death and he starts calling out, "Nurse, nurse!" And his nurse came running in the room, "What is it? What is it?" Because this is a child who could not speak above a whisper, because he was gasping for breath. And when she came in, ready to console him, [to] meet his dying needs, [Mattie] said, "Comfort the baby. The baby is crying. The baby is the future. Love the baby, because that's how life goes on." And the nurse just started crying, and she went over and she picked up the baby and she said, "Look Mattie, look, I'm loving the future. I'm holding the future for you." And . . . his body was broken, broken, bones broken, gasping, and he still was concerned about others.

Mattie did not take control of his death; instead, he chose to fully live a life of love until death came. His experience reminds me of the words of John O'Leary (whose story is told in the next chapter): "The most meaningful and truly best of life often occurs when we have the courage and humility to say yes to life, however it unfolds. It's only then we can be present for the people who need us most . . . and who we most need, too."

Those words are what make Mattie Stepanek's witness so beautiful and what make Brittany Maynard's so tragic. Even when the unfolding of life can be scary or filled with suffering, there lies a great potency within those very same moments for beauty, transformation, inspiration, and love—if we let go of control and surrender.

In fact, isn't that what Jesus teaches us in the Garden of Gethsemane? Shortly before Jesus was arrested, he went to that garden to pray. Mark says that he "began to be distressed and agitated" (Mark 14:33). He says to Peter, James, and John, "I am deeply grieved, even to death" (Mark 14:34). Luke records that "in his anguish he prayed more earnestly, and his sweat became like great drops of blood falling down on the ground" (Luke 22:44).

Then he cried out to his heavenly Father, "Abba, Father, for you all things are possible; remove this cup from me; yet, not what I want, but what you want" (Mark 14:36). The book of Matthew records that Jesus expressed this prayer of surrender to the Father's will three times (Matt. 26:39, 42, 44). Did Jesus face the utter brutality of the Crucifixion? Indeed, but he also experienced the Resurrection and, in doing so, opened the gates to eternal life.

The surrender of "Thy will be done" is something psychiatrist Dr. Elisabeth Kübler-Ross draws on in her book *Life Lessons: Two Experts on Death and Dying Teach Us About the Mysteries of Life and Living.* She writes, "Many of us labor under the illusion that control is always good, that it would be dangerous to just let the universe take care of things. But is our control really necessary to the workings of the world? We don't have to wake up early every morning to remind the universe to make the sun rise; when we turn our backs on the ocean, the universe doesn't mess up and make the tide go the wrong way. . . . To surrender we simply rise every day and say 'thy will,' not 'my will.'"

9

Not All Choices Are Equal,
But They Create a Ripple Effect
Either Way

In 1963, Rev. Martin Luther King Jr. composed his "Letter from a Birmingham Jail," in which he wrote, "We are caught in an inescapable network of mutuality, tied in a single garment of destiny. Whatever affects one directly, affects all indirectly."

Choices we make—whether big or small, positive or negative—have a permeating influence. They don't just affect us. Like a drop of food coloring in a glass of water, they diffuse into the surrounding area and impact people who, upon being touched, make other choices that in turn affect others.

The interconnectedness of our choices to other people's lives can be seen in a delightfully simple illustration: In 2013, in Newington, Connecticut, a coffee shop kept a tally of the number of customers willing to pay for the order of the patron behind him. In just a few days, *one thousand customers* participated in "paying it forward." How true it is: "Whatever affects one directly, affects all indirectly."

Or consider Zuly Sanguino, a Colombian woman who has faced profound suffering. She was born with no legs and only a portion of her arms. Her father committed suicide when she was two. She was a victim of rape. She was bullied as a child and came close to suicide in her teenage years. Now, however, she is an artist and motivational speaker who lives an incredibly full and rewarding life, sharing messages that help others.

She said, "One boy was about to take his own life with a gun when he saw a TV show I was on. He . . . decided not to take his life. He wrote to me and we're now really good friends."

How many people's lives are better because of Zuly's witness? Correspondingly, had she committed suicide (on her own or with assistance), how many people's lives would be worse (and even over) because of her absence? How true it is that we are interconnected. Our choices impact people for better—or for worse.

Consider the story of Will, a young man who was killed via the death penalty. His lawyer, David Dow, recounts Will's story in a TED talk: Will's dad left his mom while she was pregnant with Will. Will's mom, afflicted with paranoid schizophrenia, tried to kill Will with a butcher knife when he was five years old. Will was taken into the care of his brother until that brother committed suicide. By age nine, Will was living on his own. He eventually joined a gang and committed murder. The actions of Will's family members undoubtedly impacted him. There is simply no denying that we are "tied in a single garment of destiny."

Those who support assisted suicide often argue that they "have a right to autonomy" and "their choice about how to die only affects themselves." But the above stories demonstrate that this simply isn't true. As the poet John Donne once wrote, "No man is an island."

Involving medical professionals in someone's assisted suicide means another person may no longer trust a health care professional to properly care for her life. Committing assisted suicide will impact the disposition of the individual who supplies the life-ending drugs or injects the deadly poison, because you simply cannot kill another human being without that leaving a mark on your mind, your emotions, and your interactions with others. Someone getting legally endorsed assisted suicide will create a climate where another may ask for assisted suicide too—not because she truly wants it, but, as mentioned previously, because she feels "guilted" into it by a culture that embraces it and makes her feel like a useless burden. An individual's assisted suicide may influence others to respond to their own suffering and obstacles by giving up instead of turning them into opportunities (as Zuly did). How do I know this? Because "no man is an island."

Indeed, my friend Kevin Dunn demonstrates this in two documentaries he directed: *Fatal Flaws* and *The Euthanasia Deception*. In these films, he shows how the introduction of assisted suicide laws creates a slippery slope toward inevitable expansion of such killing. He shares stories of patients being asked by physicians if they want to die and of criteria broadening from being terminally ill to being simply elderly, disabled, or even depressed. He looks at countries like Belgium, where a man's grandfather had a "hastened" death that he did not request; where another man's mother who had depression was euthanized without the son knowing; and where, in a society grown accustomed to euthanasia for over a decade, complete strangers ask a family caring for their child with special needs why they did not euthanize their child. We are interconnected, and one person's assisted suicide should not be viewed in isolation but as having a ripple effect on the rest of society.

Consider the Netherlands. Their long history of allowing euthanasia and assisted suicide demonstrates how allowing *some* intentional deaths inevitably leads to more. Dr. Theo Boer was someone who had supported the Netherlands' euthanasia and assisted suicide law when it first came out, even working for almost a decade on a committee that reviewed cases. As time went on, he became increasingly troubled by what he was seeing. Now, he is known for being one of the most vocal critics of the country's law. Of its expansion, he writes, "In the pioneering years of Dutch euthanasia, it was found almost exclusively in terminally ill mentally competent adults. After some decades, the practice extended to include those with chronic conditions, disabled people, those with psychiatric problems, and incompetent adults with an advance directive. Expansion is under debate for euthanasia in young children and for elderly persons without a medical diagnosis."

Dr. Boer wrote that in 2020. By April 2023, euthanasia was set to be expanded in the Netherlands for children between the ages of one and twelve. (It is already allowed for babies under one and for children older than twelve.)

Or take my birthplace of Canada as another example. Back in 2016, Canada passed legislation that allowed for assisted suicide under certain circumstances, which it referred to as "medical assistance in dying" (MAID). But it is quickly becoming known as having one of the most liberal assisted suicide laws in the world. Consider the many ways Canada is already standing out:

- unlike anywhere else (other than some Australian states), nurse practitioners are allowed to provide MAID
- unlike the American states, provider-administered MAID is allowed
- unlike the American states, access to MAID is not limited to those who are terminally ill
- unlike the European countries, whether suffering is intolerable is assessed entirely by the person

In 2021, only five years after the initial MAID law, Canada passed new legislation that broadened access to assisted suicide, removing "the requirement for a person's natural death to be reasonably foreseeable in order to be eligible for MAID." The government's own website makes this as explicit as possible: "You do *not* need to have a fatal or terminal condition to be eligible for medical assistance in dying." Ironically, with the new law, the terminology still used is "medical *assistance in dying*," even though the government freely admits that candidates do not actually need to be considered dying.

Moreover, the country has promised to further expand access to assisted suicide with a pledge for 2024, stating that "persons suffering solely from a mental illness and who meet all other eligibility criteria will now be eligible for MAID in Canada as of March 17, 2024."

To suggest that initially allowing *some* assisted suicide in Canada leads to eventually allowing *more* is not a possibility or theory. It is a reality. It is not as if the country is at the top of a slope looking down, wondering if it is slippery; instead, it is already halfway down and picking up speed.

Just consider some personal stories. In 2022, a Canadian woman who suffered from multiple chemical sensitivities (MCS) died by assisted suicide. She was fifty-one years old. She chose that death because her life circumstances had become unbearable for her: cigarette and marijuana smoke from neighbors in her apartment building wafted into her unit, and her condition made it intolerable. Increase in chemical usage in the building for cleaning during COVID was also a significant irritation of her condition. Because of COVID restrictions, she (and the smokers in her building) spent more time confined to their units. She was miserable, and after two years of failed attempts to get government assistance with better affordable housing, she was given assisted suicide.

There have been other alarming stories, including a sixty-one-year-old man who, to the horror of his family, got suicide assistance for hearing loss, and a twenty-three-year-old young man who has diabetes and no vision in one eye who found a physician willing to give him assisted suicide, which the doctor eventually canceled when the patient's mother found out and made her outrage public on social media. There was an impoverished and disabled man who found a doctor to sign off on his application for MAID. The man was more afraid of dying homeless on the streets during a freezing Canadian winter than by assisted suicide. When people heard about his plight and responded with support, he did not follow through on his MAID application, but the fact remains that a physician had signed it. Then there is the case of a Canadian doctor who performed an act of euthanasia with no witnesses in the room, injecting a life-ending substance into a patient who chose to lie there dressed up as a clown—including wearing a wig and a red nose.

When considering the involvement of medical professionals in assisted suicide, it is worth pointing out that doctors are not baristas. Imagine going to a café to order a green tea and the barista telling you that you must have a latte. Maybe you're pregnant, and the thought of anything with espresso makes you feel nauseous. Maybe you're allergic to the milk options available. Maybe you don't like creamy drinks. Maybe you're craving green tea. Whatever your motivation, the barista's job is to offer you a selection of choices, not to dictate what you must have. The barista asks no questions about you—he simply takes your order.

Medical decisions are different. Just because a patient wants something, it does not follow that a doctor should simply fulfill the order. Physicians are trained *for years* to know the human body, its systems, pathologies that can develop, and interventions that heal. Sure, patients can take advantage of the internet and do their own research, but that is no replacement for years of formal education and clinical experience. Patients inform doctors of their symptoms and experiences so that physicians can put that through the filter of their wealth of knowledge, experience, and training. The doctor may believe multiple approaches are equivalent and explain the pros and cons of those to the patient, but the doctor objectively has more credibility to provide a robust analysis of the situation than the patient does. This does not mean that doctors are gods, nor does it mean that they can never be wrong. It also does not mean that patients are stupid. It just means that if someone knows more, they—simply put—*know more.*

So patients should not expect that they can demand things that are not medically indicated and not in their best interests; at the same time, doctors should only recommend that which is medically indicated and in a patient's best interest. Those who work in the medical profession hold much power over life. It is paramount that they steward that power responsibly and respectfully. The Hippocratic Oath gives an explicit reminder of that when it says, "I will not give a lethal drug to anyone if I am asked, nor will I advise such a plan."

Our choices should not be viewed in isolation. When one person chooses a course of action (such as a physician-assisted suicide), others in that same profession can be influenced to follow suit. The same is true when someone chooses to commit suicide: inevitably, others will follow. For example, when actor Robin Williams committed suicide in 2014, it was reported there was an increase in suicides in the subsequent five months, particularly among men.

In 2018, the World Health Organization published a document called *National Suicide Prevention Strategies*. In it they acknowledge the role that one person's suicide can have in leading others down the same road. How can we prevent such copycat behavior? They write, "Responsible reporting by the media is an essential component of suicide prevention. Media professionals should not only refrain from the glamorized presentation of cases of suicide and thereby avoid imitation by vulnerable people, but should also communicate stories of someone coping successfully, seeking and receiving help."

If suicide can lead to more suicide, we shouldn't be surprised that *assisted* suicide would lead to more assisted suicide. As mentioned earlier in this chapter, a woman who suffered from severe chemical sensitivity was given assisted suicide in Canada. After word began to spread about this, other people suffering with her same condition have also expressed interest in pursuing assisted suicide.

Then there are the numbers. Since MAID's legalization in Canada, for example, assisted suicide has been steadily increasing annually. In 2016, 1,018 people received it. Three years later, in 2019, 5,661 people received it. By 2021, that number grew again, this time to 10,064. In that year, the assisted suicide deaths were 3.3 percent of all deaths in Canada.

The Netherlands has also seen an increase in such deaths over time. In 2002, euthanasia deaths were less than 2 percent of all deaths. That rose to over 4 percent of deaths by 2019.

This is why we should not minimize the impact of our choices. Negative choices will create a negative ripple effect, while positive choices will create a positive one.

Our interconnectedness and the power of positive influence is evident in the story of John O'Leary. When John was just nine years old, the whole of his body was burned in a house fire. More than 80 percent of those burns were third degree. His chance of survival was less than half a percent. And yet today he is married, a father to four children, a motivational speaker, and an author. He not only survived; he is thriving. In his book *On Fire: The 7 Choices to Ignite a Radically Inspired Life*, John writes about the key factors that led him to the inspired life he's living today.

When John was a young boy, he was enthralled by baseball (and is to this day). His team is the St. Louis Cardinals, and he grew up listening to the baseball games on the radio. As a result, he was very familiar with the famous voice of the sportscaster for the Cardinals: Jack Buck. John revered Jack.

So just imagine young John lying on a hospital bed, strapped down, burned from head to toe, his eyes swollen shut, a ventilator in, experiencing searing pain, and not expected to survive the night.

Imagine John hearing the voice of his hero Jack—not on the radio but at his bedside, and not announcing the progress of a game but sharing words to give him a will to live. John said, "Jack Buck changed my life," and he doesn't use those words lightly. His book unfolds just how profound Jack's presence and perspective were to young John, but it all began with their encounter in the hospital in 1987.

Jack had not been a friend of the O'Learys before the fire; he had not known the family before coming to the bedside of that burned little boy from St. Louis, Missouri. Instead, he heard about John from baseball great Red Schoendienst. Red heard about John from Red's daughter Colleen. Colleen heard about John from her neighbor. Her neighbor heard about John from a friend. That friend heard about John from another friend. And that other friend was a neighbor of the O'Learys.

We humans are profoundly connected, and our decisions— even conversations—have a far-reaching effect. Thanks to a series of connections, Jack Buck's voice was the start of great things to come for John O'Leary. Jack, and many others, were pivotal players in John's road to recovery. In fact, John credits Jack for being his motivation to relearn to write: John's fingers had to be amputated because they were so badly destroyed by the fire, but when John returned home with little stubs on his hands, Jack mailed him autographed baseballs—one at a time, telling him he'd only get another if he wrote a thank you.

Jack Buck's voice was dominant in John's mind, but unfortunately, he also heard another voice that wasn't so encouraging. When John's parents took him to a hand surgeon to see if he could make what was left of the deformed hands more functional, the doctor said, "If he was a horse, I'd shoot him."

And right there is a stark lesson for all of us: By our choices and example, what "voice" do we want to be for others? The voice of hope that Jack Buck was? Or the voice of despair that the surgeon was? Both have the power of a ripple effect, but they are clearly not equal.

John's philosophy to "live inspired" is the fruit of listening to the positive voices in his life, and through that, he pays it forward to others. Our words and actions have an impact on others, and rather than embracing an attitude of despair and giving up on life that will inevitably spread to others, we ought to choose a life-affirming path that inspires others to join along.

10

Beauty and Creativity Are Transformative

A man should hear a little music, read a little poetry, and see a fine picture every day of his life, in order that worldly cares may not obliterate the sense of the beautiful which God has implanted in the human soul.

—Goethe

I love that quote. Having played the piano for more than thirty years, I have experienced the soul-stirring, beautiful power of music and believe we should always have a daily dose. In fact, some of my best talks and writings have been composed as I listened to "epic music playlist" or "movie soundtrack playlist" on YouTube. As I write this, I am listening to some of the best scores of composer Hans Zimmer.

Music cannot be touched nor seen. And yet it is one of the most powerful invisible forces in our world.

I think it's safe to say that my love of music began in the womb, since before I came along my mom had spent years as a performer, singing with her twin and a friend in a trio; that background has led her to always be humming something. With the passing of time, music became more and more a part of my life. I took singing lessons as a child and have my Grade 8 Certificate from the Royal Conservatory of Music for piano. But I would have to say my deepening love of music came out of a dark period of my life.

When my engagement ended, my thirty-fifth birthday was only six weeks away. And the plan had been for my then-fiancé's family to celebrate with my family. With that plan no longer coming to fruition, I needed to figure out an alternative so that the day didn't feel entirely depressing.

As a social butterfly who firmly believes we are made for relationship and who agrees with Dostoevsky that "beauty will save the world," the new celebration developed: go to church; have brunch with family, which included holding close my sweet two-year-old niece as I blew out my candles; have dinner with friends; and finally, one of my favorite activities: singing in the sunset amid the beauty of one of Vancouver's beaches with the sounds of my friends' harmonizing voices. When I went to bed that night, my heart was full.

Those experiences gave me joy, and I thought to myself, "Who says those should only happen once per year? Is it possible that what makes me come alive makes others come alive too? Aren't we all made for relationship, and are there others in this technology-focused culture looking for opportunities for what we were made for: union and communion, meaning human connection?" Time and again, my life has taught me that if you lead, others will follow. So after the success of "Singing in the Sunset" on my birthday, I confirmed with one of my friends that she would join me if I created a weekly summer gathering just like it. With a guarantee of one attendee, I then sent a message to a handful of friends asking if they would join for a weekly gathering beginning with going to Mass, followed by migrating to the beach and singing while God paints us a sunset. Then I circulated it to an email list. Then to a Facebook group.

And they came. Initially, there were six of us, and the numbers grew each week, sometimes up to more than thirty people. There were some who intended to come and those who we spontaneously invited because they happened to be at church beforehand. There was a three-year-old who sang an old Australian song and a seventy-five-year-old priest who did a jig and led us in a rousing chorus of "Frère Jacques." There was a stranger who joined us after his nearby game of volleyball and Chinese tourists walking past who, in broken English, requested we sing "Country Roads" because it was the only song they knew in English. The gathering started out with one guitar, and eventually a whole family of instruments made their way to our party: a mandolin, ukuleles, shakers, drums, a toy flute, and—going really exotic here—a didgeridoo. We praised God with "How Great Thou Art" and rocked out to "The Lion Sleeps Tonight."

It. Was. Amazing.

I am quite confident that I would not have organized any of this had I not found myself in such difficult circumstances. Wedding planning is what I had in mind for that summer—not shattered dreams. But even from unexpected and painful situations, God's grace can bring about new experiences of joy. When one chapter ends sadly, it doesn't mean there aren't other good—even great—chapters to be written.

The whole experience reminded me of this quote I once heard: "Hope is like a bird that senses the dawn and carefully starts to sing even while it is still dark."

For those who feel surrounded by darkness, how can we help them turn the light on? When someone feels that dying is better than living, what beauty can we introduce into their world?

Music is an invisible power that can turn light on in darkness and bring beauty to a world of ugliness. Music stirs the heart; it lifts the spirits; it soothes the soul; it unlocks memories.

The documentary *Alive Inside* demonstrates this. It shares the story of a social worker who visits elderly people with dementia living in care homes. He finds out what music individual patients listened to in their younger years and creates a personalized playlist. What he discovers is that people who had lost so much of their memories could nonetheless recall lyrics from decades prior. What he learns is that those who present externally as being lifeless are actually "alive inside" when familiar songs are reintroduced into their world. People smiled, sang along, and even danced. By his example, he teaches us that our gift to these individuals is not to lead them out of the world through assisted suicide but rather to allow ourselves to be led into theirs. Music does that in a powerful way.

Dementia is one condition that leads some people to believe that assisted suicide is the answer. "After all," they wonder, "who would want to live in such a miserable state?" In response, I think of my friend Nicole Scheidl, who created an organization called Fit Minds as a way of helping people with dementia. On their website, they write, "Our vision is to give unprecedented support to seniors to be all they can be. We provide customized cognitive coaching to . . . build cognitive resilience. Our mission is to slow the advancement of dementia, improve the quality of life for seniors, create hope and meaningful relationships and use our business to bring joy to seniors."

Fit Minds and *Alive Inside* are proof that meeting suffering with beauty and creativity can transform those involved and open up new horizons.

I saw the truth of this before my very eyes. As a result of a couple summers of "Sunset Singing," I was not content just to sing: I wanted to play an instrument too. But I also knew that bringing my piano to the beach was simply not a possibility. With several friends showing up with ukuleles, I thought to myself, "Four strings? Super small! I can learn that!" And so began my love affair with the uku- lele, an instrument I now play more than my piano. When I travel at airports with its case on my back, strangers will often approach and ask, "Is that a violin?" My favorite response is to say, "No—it's even better. It's a ukulele." That usually elicits a surprised look, to which I respond, "A violin is inherently sad. But the ukulele is like the accordion: it's an inherently happy instrument!" And inevitably, the person smiles.

Playing the ukulele is not only a joy for me but has also become a gift I give to others (including to my Uber drivers who have en- joyed my free "concerts"). I have had the opportunity to play and sing for all kinds of people, including a sick elderly woman who said, "When I hear the music my pain goes away."

On another occasion, I played for a woman with dementia, and when I began with "You are my . . ." she immediately chimed in "sunshine! My only sunshine . . ." She clearly hadn't forgotten everything.

I have seen music literally move people to tears. One particularly poignant encounter was with an older gentleman who requested the song my little nephew always asks me to play: Johnny Cash's "Ring of Fire." Needless to say, I was happy to oblige. I got only two lines in when he began to weep. I slowed down and gently asked, "Do you want me to stop, or do you want me to keep going?" I knew that music had power to flood the mind with memories and, even if these were painful, sometimes people want to "stay there" for a moment, to feel again. This man did; he told me to keep going.

When I eventually brought the song to its end, I looked at his tear-stained face and softly said, "Music can stir in our hearts deep emotions. I can see this song did that for you. Do you want to share about it?"

And so began an hour-plus conversation, where he talked about broken relationships and painful regret, about walls built around the heart and the power of love to break them down, about connection, loss, contribution, and admiration; in short, we talked about his journey of life and all the burdens he was still carrying in his heart. Music became the door to this expression, release, and processing.

Instead of assisting people with suicide, we should ask, "How can we assist them with processing their past and moving forward with hope? And how can beauty be an instrument for accomplishing that?"

We should work, for example, at making environments more aesthetically pleasing. Secondhand stores have a wide selection of canvas and other beautiful art that is economical and that we could use for decorating places in which the sick and elderly spend a lot of time. Flowers always brighten a room, and carnations are an inexpensive kind that last a long time.

I think of what my cousin did to surround herself with beauty when she was very sick. Belinda, who I referenced in chapter 3 (who surprised me by redecorating my basement suite), has faced many health challenges. The latest was in December 2018, when she had major chest surgery as well as a hysterectomy (removal of the uterus) and the removal of the fallopian tubes, an ovary, and the cervix. This was because she had endometriosis not only in her pelvis but also, incredibly, in her chest cavity. This debilitating and rare condition (called thoracic endometriosis) meant that when her uterus bled cyclically, so did cells inside her chest cavity. It resulted in ten episodes of a collapsed lung and four thoracic lung surgeries. All that unknowingly began when Belinda was seven weeks pregnant with her son and contracted H1N1 and had a three-liter fluid collection around her right lung. When her lung was drained, the needle punctured her diaphragm, creating a hole that was stretched by that pregnancy and the next, resulting in her liver herniating through her diaphragm into her thoracic (chest) cavity. This created an entrance for the endometriosis where cells from the uterus migrated through the diaphragm into her chest cavity. Before this was discovered, she was diagnosed with rheumatoid arthritis, which causes great pain in her wrists, hands, knees, toes, and cervical spine. When the thoracic endometriosis was eventually discovered and she had all the surgeries, she also dealt with complications afterward, such as a bowel obstruction after one surgery and pneumonia after another.

Needless to say, those years of her life involved much suffering and many hospitalizations. And yet, she was very intentional about beauty and creativity in an otherwise depressing time. She had her husband pack her cozy duvet from home to avoid the ugly, thin hospital blanket. When I would tuck her in at night, she had me spray lavender essential oil around her in order to mask the various hospital smells. She had a morning routine that helped her feel fresh and energized: a new set of pajamas for the day that were different from what she slept in and makeup application. ("Look better, feel better" was her philosophy.) Handmade pictures from her children decorated her room. She even brought a fine-bone china teacup from home in order to drink tea from that instead of the hospital's blue plastic mug. And, of course, a continuous stream of family and friends helped move her painful days along. These were all little things, but they made a big difference.

Beauty. Creativity. These are what we should aspire toward, not assisted suicide.

When I think of the power of creativity as part of our response to the sick, I immediately think of Dr. Paul Brand. As a child of missionaries, he grew up in India. He moved to England to attend medical school, and it was during World War II that he became a physician. He then returned to India to work as a doctor, specifically to serve people with leprosy (also called Hansen's disease).

Dr. Brand, a hand surgeon, came to realize that leprosy was a problem of nerves, not tissue—that the breakdown of fingers and toes, for example, was not because leprosy was "eating away" at them but because a leper's inability to feel pain caused him or her to unwittingly do self-destructive things. In his book *The Gift of Pain: Why We Hurt & What We Can Do About It*, coauthored by Philip Yancey, he cites a case of a woman cooking a yam over a fire. When the yam accidentally fell off a stick, Dr. Brand watched in horror as the woman called for a person nearby who had leprosy to reach his hand into the burning hot coals to retrieve the yam. Because he felt no pain, he didn't think twice about subjecting his limb to such devastating destruction.

Dr. Brand responded to the plight of leprosy patients by unleashing creativity: performing restorative hand surgeries and teaching patients how to be consciously careful when doing various activities, as well as how to check their bodies for signs of sores.

He learned to unleash even more creativity when some of his patients returned to him after he had restored their hands to an aesthetically pleasing and functional state. One patient said, "Dr. Brand, these are not good hands"—a sentiment he was to discover that other patients felt too. The patient explained that his previously deformed hands had been an asset when he begged. Now that his hands were repaired, he no longer succeeding in making enough money to provide for his needs. But finding work was also not an option because leprosy had left his face with scars and markings that deterred people from employing him.

Dr. Brand reflected,

> My stomach twisted in a knot as John told me of the rejection he had encountered in the outside world. When he tried to board a public bus, sometimes the driver would physically throw him off. He, an educated man, was now unemployed and homeless, sleeping in an open plaza. He barely earned enough money from his begging to buy food. What had I done, repaired his body just enough to ruin his last chance for a livelihood? . . .

> In order to equip leprosy patients for life on the "outside," we would have to change our approach radically. We must lift our

sights from the narrow field of surgery on hands and feet and bring the whole person into view.

Dr. Brand had the ears to hear what his patient was ultimately communicating and had the eyes to see the bigger picture. When John said, "These are not good hands," what he was really expressing was this: *Fixing my hands has not entirely fixed my problem. Please help me.*

And so, rather than undo the surgery he had done, rather than maim his patients so that they could better beg, Dr. Brand got creative and performed surgery to transfer hair from the scalp to above the eyes in order to re-grow eyebrows for leprosy patients who had lost theirs. He also did plastic surgery to reconstruct the sunken noses many sufferers of the condition were marred with. By doing this, he removed the obvious signs of having had leprosy and opened the door to new opportunities for his patients.

Dr. Brand's wife, Margaret, was equally creative. Also a physician, she worked in ophthalmology and was deeply troubled that a majority of leprosy patients experienced damage to their eyes. Blindness was a troubling and frightening reality for many.

Have you ever had a staring contest with a friend and tried not to blink? Eventually, both parties cave, often declaring as they fight back the urge to close their eyelids, "Ouch! That hurts." After a while, not blinking hurts. But what if you cannot feel the hurt? Then you won't blink, as was the case for many leprosy patients who lost pain sensation in their eyes. But not blinking meant that such a person's eyes would dry out and be more likely to develop damage and ulceration. (Again, just think about when you get something like a dust particle in your eye: it hurts, so you blink and try to get it out. But people with leprosy won't feel that pain; with dust and other irritants not consciously aggravating them, the eye won't respond in a protective way.)

Dr. Brand wrote of his wife, "Early on, Margaret saw a vivid illustration of the kind of abuse that can happen to a patient whose eyes are insensitive to pain: a man reached up and vigorously rubbed his open eyes with a hand covered with huge, crusty calluses. Little wonder her patients were going blind!"

When Dr. Margaret failed at teaching her leprosy patients to consciously think of blinking, she came up with another solution: she implemented the surgical technique of Sir Harold Gillies. "It involved detaching one end of part of the temporalis muscle, which controls clenching of the jaw and chewing, and connecting it to a strand of fascia running through the eyelids." And so, when her patients chewed gum, or food, their eyelids would blink, providing the much-needed lubrication for the surface of the eyes.

The Brands' creativity led to all kinds of fascinating innovations. For example, Dr. Paul added "cat breeder" to his resume in response to another problem he discovered: some leprosy sufferers were coming to him and reporting that they were waking up with parts of their fingers or toes missing after sleeping. Dr. Brand was confused about how this would happen when the patient was at rest. One night, as a patient slept, a fellow patient noticed a rat climb onto the bed and go up to the man's finger. Because he did not have sensation, he did not react, and the rat began to chew the flesh of the patient. Of course, the observer's screams intervened and put an end to the rodent's feast. But the problem was identified. Dr. Brand's creative solution? Breed cats and send one home with each of his leprosy patients so that they had a cat to sleep with, which would ward off rodents.

The suffering of the Brands' patients was profound. But never was the Brands' solution to end their patients' lives. Instead, it was to get creative and find new, out-of-the-box ways to end their patients' suffering. Similarly, when someone says, "I want assisted suicide," the task of a truly caring individual is to hear what is being communicated but not verbalized, to search for what is underneath their request, to see the bigger picture, and to get creative about a life-affirming response.

Moreover, there is a deeper message we can take away from the Brands than just the power of creativity. Their work teaches us something we might initially recoil at: Pain matters. Pain is important. Pain is a *gift*. Why? Because pain is a messenger. Certainly, we shouldn't leave someone in a pain-riddled state (just think about the excruciating condition of EB mentioned in chapter 4), but we should listen to it. Simply put, pain (whether physical, emotional, psychological, or spiritual) is telling us that something is wrong. People with leprosy teach us that when we do not feel pain, all kinds of destructive things happen to us and hurt us more than pain itself. So when we do feel pain and anguish, it's an opportunity to ask, "What is this pain an indicator of? Is emotional pain a sign that I have closed people out of my life? Is it a sign that I have been traumatized in my past and yet to deal with something? Is physical pain a sign of cancer growing that, if not felt, would be a silent killer?" There are endless reasons for the various pains we may encounter, but when we feel pain, rather than run to assisted suicide, we should pause and explore what pain is telling us and then respond with beauty and creativity.

Myra Brooks Welch captured this idea in a poem composed almost a hundred years ago. She has the reader imagine an auction where an old violin is up for sale. The instrument is so battered and dusty that the auctioneer's attempts to entice a buyer prove futile. But then an old man steps forward. He wipes away the dust. He tunes the strings. And he plays a sweet melody.

After that, the auctioneer tries once more to sell the violin and does so at an amount *three thousand times* the original asking price.

The awed audience wonders what made the difference. And someone cries out (as the poem is aptly titled), "The touch of the Master's hand."

How often do people, like the Brands' patients, feel like the old violin? How often do sickness, disease, disability, and suffering make one feel like a worthless instrument to be rejected rather than prized? Assisted suicide feeds that false narrative. Instead, we are affirmed when we surrender ourselves "to the touch of the Master's hand" who uses creativity and beauty to make "all things new" (Rev. 21:5).

Epilogue

"Some people come into our lives and quickly go. Some stay
for a while and leave footprints on our hearts and we are never,
ever the same."
—*Flavia and the Dream Maker: The Musical*

My friend Alex is one such person who left footprints on my heart.
Interestingly, my encounters with him were few, but the impact
was lasting. Our first meeting was in 2013 during a family meal
along with his wife, Elaine, their young children, Samuel and Esther
(ages four and two, respectively), and a couple of their friends. I
had just made a short-term move to Eastern Canada, and, knowing
about my pro-life work, they had demonstrated their charism of
hospitality and welcomed me to their home.

What struck me most that night was how gentle they all were.
It was a beautiful demonstration of the passage from Colossians
3:15: "Let the peace of Christ rule in your hearts." There was a
tangible and profound serenity radiating from each of them. It was
remarkable and would be something I experienced in subsequent
encounters.

Only a few months after that first meeting, Alex would be diagnosed with brain cancer. He was thirty-four.

For the next five years, Alex was like a candle: he burned brightly. In between brain surgeries, he even edited a major writing project for me, making significant improvements and helpful editorial contributions. And yet, as all wicks eventually dwindle, sadly Alex's time in this world would too. Shortly before his fortieth birthday, Alex's earthly pilgrimage came to an end.

I was part of a group of friends and family who regularly received email updates from Alex over the years of his cancer journey. What always struck me was his disposition. Never was he angry at God. Instead, he lived day by day, praying he would live to see his children's children, believing God could heal him, and trusting—regardless of whether his prayers were answered as he wished—that God was good.

With Elaine's permission, I have included a few of Alex's messages sent in the final year and a half of his life. Alex's words are part of his rich legacy. They are a beacon for each of us, illuminating a perspective for how to live—and how to die. By his example, Alex taught me what I hope this book has taught you: to treasure the gift of life for as long as we are given it, to use our time to love and be loved, and to live in submission to our heavenly Father whose ways are not ours.

July 24, 2017

Beloved,

Yesterday, marked the fourth year since God's right hand began specifically sustaining me under the prognosis of brain cancer. It was 4 years ago, yesterday, when I suffered a seizure in the parking lot of [a mall], leaving me unconscious. Samuel was 4 years old. Esther was 2. Both were strapped into their stroller that morning. Both were protected by the Lord through the first-responder on the scene, a police officer.

I was rushed to [the] hospital where a 5cm mass was found. . . . I was transferred to [another hospital]. After undergoing brain surgery, I learned that the tumor was too invasive to remove. Second, I would come to learn that the tumor was malignant. Third, I would learn that God is faithful to supply what is needed for each day.

Four years ago, I did not anticipate that I would be writing this update. I did not anticipate that I'd have celebrated Samuel's 8th birthday with him. I did not anticipate that Elaine and I would be planning Esther's 6th birthday. Four years ago, I did not anticipate that Elaine and I would be preparing to celebrate our 11th wedding anniversary. Each of these milestones is an unspeakable manifestation of God's kindness to me.

So, on this day, I simply want to update you that my heart rejoices in God my Savior for He has done great and mighty deeds. Holy is His name!

I love Jesus today more than I ever have. He is my beloved and I am His. I know He loves me. Though medically my future may be uncertain, His love endures forever.

With love, Alex

September 20, 2017

Beloved, a couple of weeks ago, my pastor preached from Psalm 150. This Psalm is a psalm (song) of praise. Its final verse says, "Let everything that has breath praise the Lord" (Psalm 150:6). Since I have breath, I am included in this command. Regardless of my physical condition, allow me to praise the Lord.

1. I praise the Lord because He is the one who forgives all sins and heals all diseases (Psalm 103:3–4).
2. I praise the Lord for competent and compassionate medical professionals who are using their education and experience to work for my health and my care.
3. I praise the Lord that though my Avastin treatments were extremely expensive, the Lord provided a grant to help offset some of the cost of the treatments. Without my knowledge, my medical team applied for this grant. I only found out after I had been selected to receive it.
4. I praise the Lord for my team of therapists at [the rehabilitation center] where I am receiving specialized physiotherapy and occupational therapy. I praise the Lord for these

professionals who are patient with me as I relearn how to walk and how to write.

5. I praise the Lord for the freedom I have to grieve and feel sadness. Watching Samuel and Esther grow up and not being able to physically participate in all that they are involved does bring me sadness. Yet, I praise the Lord that he invites me to express that sorrow to him and I have often taken up that invitation.

6. I praise the Lord for Elaine who continues to maintain the home with grace and charity despite my limitations.

7. I praise the Lord for the body of Christ in different spheres of my life—who support me and stand with me in many practical ways: by praying for me and my family, driving me to appointments, mowing the lawn, preparing meals and sharing out of their abundance.

8. I praise the Lord for mornings spent with my children, reading the Bible and praying before they head off for school.

9. I praise the Lord for different family and friends who have moved into the house to help care for me for a season and to give Elaine a hand with day-to-day tasks.

10. I praise the Lord for my school community where Elaine and I teach and where Samuel and Esther study . . . and the love, care and support that it has offered me and my family during this season in our lives.

As I bring this update to a close, I invite you to join me in praising God for all his benefits. On Thursday, Sept. 21, I will have an MRI to see how the first two infusions of Avastin have worked. Please pray for a good report which will allow me to return to work as soon as possible.

Also pray for the restoration of my fine motor skills. I am having to relearn how to write. It is certainly humbling to be learning the same things as my 6 year old daughter!

Thank you for standing with me in prayer. I look forward to giving you a good report of answered prayer.

With sincere love, Alex

April 6, 2018

Beloved,

Grace and peace to you in Jesus Christ.

By God's grace, I was able to return to work on a part-time basis at the beginning of February, and have been blessed to be teaching and ministering . . . once again.

However, today we had some difficult news during an MRI follow up. I have been experiencing increased weakness and coldness in my left hand and foot. Doctors ruled out the possibility of blood clots, but seem to think that the tumor is now progressing. This is concerning, since we are presently using the last available treatment option.

While I will continue with my present treatment for now in order to slow down this progression, the doctors are suggesting that I focus on making the most of my time with my family, since the prognosis does not look promising.

Please continue to lift us up in prayer, that God would heal me, strengthen me and lengthen my life by decades so that I will see my children's children. Pray for our children and for God's wisdom for us to discern what to tell them and when.

Here is a reflection I wrote. Please pray that the remaining days/decades of my life would be invested in what is crucial, not what is trivial:

A matter or issue which is "crucial" is one which is extremely important. The root of "crucial" is "crucis"—the cross. I find it significant that in English, when a person wishes to indicate that something is extremely important, they have to refer to the cross. It was the apostle Paul, writing to Corinthian Christians who said, "For I handed on to you as of first importance what I also received: that Christ died for our sins in accordance with the scriptures; that He was buried; that He was raised on the third day in accordance with the scriptures; that He appeared to Kephas, then to the Twelve" (1 Corinthians 15:3–5). If "first importance" is synonymous with "crucial" then Paul is essentially saying that what is ultimately crucial is the "crucis," where Jesus died in the place of a sinner like me, His burial and His resurrection. This is what is "crucial."

Father in heaven, I ask that my life be invested in what is literally crucial—the death, burial and resurrection of your Son. In Jesus' name, Amen.

With love, Alex

June 19, 2018

Beloved in Christ,

Thank you for your ongoing support and your steadfast love shown to me and my family.

Since the end of April, I have been spending time at home with Elaine. We have also been keeping the children home two days a week, so that we can enjoy time as a family.

I am showing signs of increasing physical weakness and the most recent MRI revealed significant tumor growth. As a result, I have discontinued my treatments, but my faith in Jesus remains unshaken. We look to him each day as our joy and strength. Though my outward body is wasting away, my joy in Jesus Christ increases and the peace I know is beyond understanding.

I have been meditating on the Hebrews as they left Egypt. From their perspective, with every step they took away from Egypt and towards the Red Sea, the Hebrews must have surmised that they were proceeding towards their ultimate demise, especially with the Egyptian army behind them. From God's perspective, God knew that with every step they took away from Egypt and towards the Red Sea, the Hebrews were proceeding towards their ultimate deliverance regardless of the Egyptian army behind them. In the same way, I know that with each passing day, I am moving closer to my ultimate deliverance and for this I am grateful.

We have had many visitors coming in and out of our house and I've had the opportunity to share with them the encouragement I find in Psalm 103. I regularly find myself reading and meditating on this Psalm. . . .

Along with praying for me, I would covet your prayers for Elaine. She is carrying a heavy load emotionally and a heavy load physically. One year ago, there were two pairs of hands to maintain the home. Now it is Elaine who has to maintain the home largely on her own. She needs physical, emotional and spiritual strength for each new day.

Also, pray for Samuel and Esther, now nine and almost seven. They are fully aware of all that is transpiring and I desire that they will not grow bitter towards the Lord as they observe what is happening. Please pray that the outcome of this season in our lives will see them with gentle and tender hearts towards the Lord.

God bless, Alex

September 10, 2018

Dear Friends and Family,

We are so grateful to God for all of you and the love and support you have shown us.

We wanted to update you on Alex's health, and to ask for your continued prayers for our family. Alex was recently admitted to [the] hospital . . . where a scan confirmed further swelling and probable tumor progression. The doctor put him onto a very high dose of steroids, which is intended to improve his symptoms for a period of time.

The steroids have improved these initial symptoms. However, Alex is weak and his mobility is very restricted. . . . At this point we are remaining in the hospital, where we are receiving excellent care from a compassionate and competent medical team.

Please uphold Alex in your prayers. Pray that he would know God's healing power, and sense God's joy and peace daily. Pray that the children would have peace in a very difficult and busy time, as I am rushing between the hospital and home each day. Pray that God would grant me strength and peace also as I seek to bless and assist Alex at this time. A verse I have found so much comfort in this summer comes from Isaiah 30:15 . . . "In repentance and rest is your salvation, in quietness and trust is your strength."

We seek to rest and trust in the goodness of God, and look to him as our strength and salvation.

Sending love to you all, Elaine and Alex, Samuel and Esther

November 4, 2018

Dearest Family and Friends,

Early this morning, around 4am, Alex passed peacefully into the arms of Jesus. . . . We could not have asked for a more gracious closure to his life.

We are so thankful for each of your prayers, and for the encouragement and care you have provided for us on this journey. Praise God, that even in death, we have hope in Christ:

"Do not let your hearts be troubled. You have faith in God; have faith also in me. In my Father's house there are many dwelling places. If there were not, would I have told you that I am going to prepare a place for you?" (John 14:1–2).

With much love, Elaine

If anyone had faith that he could be healed, Alex did. And yet, God did not heal him—that is, on this side of heaven. Alex never wavered in his love of the Lord, even as his wish to live to see his children's children would not come to fruition—at least, as we comprehend it.

I wrote Elaine, now left widowed to parent their two young children alone. I asked her, "Alex had such faith that God would heal him. How have you worked through the reality that he didn't? What advice do you have for people who have the same hope and may experience the same disappointment? Did you ever get angry at God? Why or why not?"

In her beautifully tender way, Elaine wrote,

One of the marked challenges I faced along this journey was how to interact with the people who kept insisting that if we simply trusted in faith, then God would heal. Alex himself would often cling to Bible verses that spoke of God's healing. I had no doubt that God could heal, but came to see that our posture of prayer should be like that of the woman who simply reached out her hand and grabbed hold of Jesus' cloak, knowing that power rested in Him. We must similarly stretch out our hands in eager expectation, knowing God can do miracles, but also recognizing that this side of heaven, sickness and death often remain. Until we reach heaven, we cannot claim complete health. Scripture says too much about suffering to allow for that. So our task is to boldly ask and then to wait upon the God who may heal now and who may heal in the life to come.

I am grateful that long before this journey began I had wrestled through this question of suffering and had been led to some truths that have shaped the way I viewed God in the midst of our great loss. While Scripture does not give us all the answers about a particular trial we endure, we can remember that the bookends of Scripture are paradise. God created a perfect world without sin or sickness, and is creating a world in which those things will be eradicated forever. But that is not all! In the middle of the story, where we humans suffer and grieve, Jesus came and met us in his own broken body, suffering not only with us but for us. That he suffers with us gives comfort for the heartaches we face. That he suffers for us gives us hope for the life to come.

I could have ended this book with an epic story of someone who suffered, prayed for healing, and experienced a miracle. And while such a narrative can serve a beautiful purpose to show what *is* possible, it can also leave those who don't experience such a "happily ever after" feeling disappointed and unable to relate—perhaps even feeling left out. Even those who do experience miracles will, in other ways, still suffer, for suffering is the universal human experience. Because of that, we need a universal human response.

Humans are designed for connection and love, but suicide assistance disconnects and robs us of the very lives through which we love. And so, an opportunity lies before all of us, who are each in the middle of our own unique stories. And that opportunity is to illuminate the brighter path that is the alternative to suicide assistance. That path entails the quiet strength of surrender, an emphasis on beauty and creativity, and a focus on loving relationships. At the heart of it all is to "start with what" and to seek, and find, meaning in any circumstance. When we do that, we will bring to life these words of Léon Bloy: "There are places in the heart that do not yet exist; suffering has to enter in for them to come to be."

Notes

EPIGRAPH

v   **"God blessed the broken road"**: "God Bless the Broken Road" by Rascal Flatts.

INTRODUCTION

3   **"In the crushing, in the pressing, you are making new wine"**: Brooke Ligertwood, "New Wine," Hillsong Music Publishing, 2017, https://hillsong.com/lyrics/new-wine/.

4   **"Why US Suicide Rate Is on the Rise"**: Ritu Prasad, "Why US Suicide Rate Is on the Rise," BBC News, June 11, 2018, https://www.bbc.co.uk/news/world-us-canada-44416727.

4   **"Suicide Rates Sharply Increase Among Girls"**: Robert Glatter, "Suicide Rates Sharply Increase Among Girls," *Forbes*, May 20, 2019, https://www.forbes.com/sites/robertglatter/2019/05/20/suicide-rates-sharply-increase-among-young-girls-study-finds/.

4   **"Suicide Deaths Reached a Record High in the US in 2022"**: Deidre McPhillips, "Suicide Deaths Reached a Record High in the US in 2022, Provisional Data Shows," CNN, August 10, 2023, https://www.cnn.com/2023/08/10/health/suicide-deaths-record-high-2022/index.html#:~:text=At%20least%2049%2C449%20lives%20were,the%20previous%20record%20from%202018.

5   **a growing number of states allow assisted suicide**: "World Map," World Federation Right to Die Societies website, accessed November 22, 2023, https://wfrtds.org/worldmap/.

5   **major world religions make stories a core part of their teachings**: *Religions of the World* series, BBC, accessed November 22, 2023, https://www.bbc.co.uk/programmes/articles/1pYRg2f202rqWHrp3ywhTyX/religions-of-the-world.

6   **"Gentleness and kind persuasion win where force and bluster fail"**: "The North Wind & the Sun," in *The Aesop for Children*, Library of Congress website, http://read.gov/aesop/143.html.

CHAPTER I

8   **Matt has turned suffering into a source of meaning:** Information about Matt is available at the Matt Hampson Foundation website, https://www.matthampsonfoundation .org/who-we-are/meet-matt-hampson.

8   **"We can get busy living, or get busy dying":** TEDx Talks, "#GETBUSY LIVING," YouTube video, November 22, 2016, https://www.youtube.com/watch?v=wWdwP31Ux-g. Note: Those words are also from the movie *The Shawshank Redemption.*

9   **Dan was so overwhelmed that he attempted suicide:** Jeremy Laurance, "Agony of Helping a Son to Kill Himself," *The Independent*, May 27, 2011, https://www.independent .co.uk/life-style/health-and-families/health-news/agony-of-helping-a-son-to-kill -himself-2289710.html.

9   **This culminated in him traveling to Switzerland:** Anna Davis, "Father Tells How Paralysed Rugby Son Took Poison in Swiss Flat," *Evening Standard*, April 12, 2012, https:// www.standard.co.uk/news/father-tells-how-paralysed-rugby-son-took-poison-in-swiss -flat-6905536.html.

9   **a life of paralysis is a cross of tremendous weight:** It is worth pointing out something my friend Alex Schadenberg drew my attention to. Alex has spent two decades educating people on euthanasia through his organization Euthanasia Prevention Coalition, and through his blog he shared insight from Gordon Friesen, who wrote, "Only somewhat less than one percent of the victims of spinal cord injuries will despair, renounce, and end their lives during the first crucial five years of recovery (and after that time, their specific suicide rates become statistically identical to those of the general population)" (Friesen, "Who Really Wants to Die? Part V: The Absence of Suicidal Desire amongst the Survivors of Catastrophic Injury," Euthanasia Prevention Coalition website, September 21, 2020, https://alexschadenberg.blogspot.com/2020/09/normal-0-false-false-false-fr-ca-x-none .html). This is important to show that suicide is not the "normal" response to paralysis or disability in general. Obviously legalizing euthanasia / assisted suicide will change that statistic, but it is important we realize that it is not the condition itself that is the greatest threat to these individuals but rather a societal concept of a "life unworthy of life."

9   **complications from paralysis:** "Living with Paralysis: Secondary Conditions," Christopher & Dana Reeve Foundation website, accessed November 22, 2023, https://www .christopherreeve.org/living-with-paralysis/health/secondary-conditions.

9   **"despair is suffering without meaning":** "Finding meaning in difficult times (Interview with Dr. Viktor Frankl)," YouTube video, October 28, 2011, https://www .youtube.com/watch?v=LlC2OdnhIiQ.

10   it is despair that can lead to suicide: This section draws from my article "Finding Meaning in Suffering," *Love Unleashes Life* blog, December 7, 2016, https://loveunleashes life.com/blog/2016/12/6/finding-meaning-in-suffering-by-stephanie-gray.

10   Dr. Frankl cites a teenager in Texas: "Interview with Dr. Viktor Frankl."

10   "I broke my neck but it did not break me": "Interview with Dr. Viktor Frankl."

10   "They can mold . . . their predicament into an accomplishment": "Interview with Dr. Viktor Frankl."

11   Simon Sinek teaches people to "start with why": Sinek has given one of the most popular TED talks of all time ("How Great Leaders Inspire Action"), which is based on his book *Start with Why*, where he proposes the importance of knowing one's reasons, one's "why," in order to achieve great businesses, influence, and social change.

12   Patrick John and Patrick Henry Hughes: Information is taken from an ESPN story from 2006 available on YouTube ("Patrick Henry Hughes," YouTube video, February 3, 2009, https://www.youtube.com/watch?v=9xwCG0Ey2Mg).

13   When Patrick wrote a book, it was his father who coauthored it with him: Their book is called *I Am Potential: Eight Lessons on Living, Loving, and Reaching Your Dreams*.

13   *The Lord of the Rings* even "starts with what": *Lord of the Rings: The Fellowship of the Ring*, directed by Peter Jackson (New Line Cinema, 2001). Emphasis added.

13   Michael Morton: Learn about Michael in his memoir *Getting Life: An Innocent Man's 25-Year Journey from Prison to Peace, A Memoir*, his website michael-morton.com, and the documentary *An Unreal Dream: The Michael Morton Story*, 2013.

14   The Innocence Project: Learn more about The Innocence Project at https://www .innocenceproject.org/, and learn about their role in Michael's case at https://www .innocenceproject.org/cases/michael-morton/.

15   "Even though I would have liked nothing better": Michael Morton, *Getting Life: An Innocent Man's 25-Year Journey from Prison to Peace, A Memoir* (New York: Simon & Schuster, 2014), 233.

15   my friend Lisa: Read Lisa's writings on her blog, *The Resilient Catholic*, https:// resilientcatholic.home.blog/author/resilientlisa/.

16   my friends Peter and Anne: Not their real names.

17   **"The more one forgets himself"**: Viktor Frankl, *Man's Search for Meaning* (Boston: Beacon, 1992), 115.

CHAPTER 2

20   **Berthia had struggled with severe depression:** TEDx Talks, "The Impact of Listening," YouTube video, July 27, 2015, https://www.youtube.com/watch?v=HB2_lA68YDU.

20   **Briggs responded to a call about a possible suicide attempt:** TED, "The Bridge between Suicide and Life," YouTube video, May 14, 2014, https://www.youtube.com/watch?time_continue=574&v=7CIq4mtiamY.

21   **More than two hundred people are alive today because of Briggs:** Josh K. Elliott, "San Francisco's 'Golden Gate Guardian' prevented more than 200 suicides," CTV News, March 26, 2018, https://www.ctvnews.ca/health/san-francisco-s-golden-gate-guardian-prevented-more-than-200-suicides-1.3858896.

21   **"Who gets suicide prevention and who gets suicide assistance?":** Blaise Alleyne and Jonathon Van Maren, *A Guide to Discussing Assisted Suicide* (Toronto: Life Cycle Books, 2017), eBook version.

22   **"Most people who support assisted suicide also support suicide prevention":** Alleyne and Van Maren.

23   **the heart of the belief system of civil societies:** This section is taken from a booklet I wrote for The Chilliwack Pro-Life Society, *An FAQ about Euthanasia and Assisted Suicide*, available at https://loveunleasheslife.com/s/Euthanasia-FAQ.pdf/.

23   **"Recognition of the inherent dignity":** United Nations General Assembly, "Universal Declaration of Human Rights," 1948, https://www.un.org/en/about-us/universal-declaration-of-human-rights.

26   **Consider the 1994 Rwandan genocide:** This section is taken from my article "The Second-Last Word," *Love Unleashes Life* blog, October 23, 2017, https://loveunleasheslife.com/blog/2017/10/23/the-second-last-word-by-stephanie-gray.

26   **Rwandan genocide survivor Monica:** "The Story of Monica, a Hutu Survivor," International Alert website, May 2014, https://www.international-alert.org/stories/story-monica-hutu-survivor.

26 **Penny Boudreau:** Susan Bradley, "Penny Boudreau, Who Killed Her Daughter, to Get Escorted Leaves from Prison," CBC News, July 5, 2018, https://www.cbc.ca/news /canada/nova-scotia/penny-boudreau-murder-daughter-escorted-leaves-prison-1.4735247.

29 **assisted suicide because she is suffering from fibromyalgia:** Avis Favaro and Elizabeth St. Philip, "This Woman with an Incurable Disorder Wants to End Her Life, But Can't Get Assisted Death," CTV News, December 8, 2019, https://www.ctvnews.ca/health /this-woman-with-an-incurable-disorder-wants-to-end-her-life-but-can-t-get-assisted -death-1.4720730.

30 **How does one decide how close to death a person must be?:** Points in this section taken from my article "Assisted Suicide in Select Cases?" *Love Unleashes Life* blog, May 8, 2017, https://loveunleasheslife.com/blog/2017/5/8/assisted-suicide-in-select-cases -by-stephanie-gray.

31 **"sweeping controls on the distribution of its products":** Eric Eckholm, "Pfizer Blocks the Use of Its Drugs in Executions," *The New York Times*, May 13, 2016, https:// www.nytimes.com/2016/05/14/us/pfizer-execution-drugs-lethal-injection.html?_r=1.

31 **"requiring physicians to participate in executions":** "NEW VOICES: American Medical Association, EMT Association Say Participation in Executions Violates Medical Ethics," Death Penalty Information Center website, July 18, 2006, https://deathpenalty info.org/node/1775.

31 **Couldn't the same be said about health care workers' involvement in assisted suicide?:** Connors, "Assisted Suicide in Select Cases?"

32 **"Suicide ends one life, and it affects so many others":** Kevin Briggs, *Guardian of the Golden Gate: Protecting the Line Between Hope and Despair* (Overland Park, KS: Ascend Books, 2015), 113.

32 **"Hope is the single most important tool":** Briggs, 281.

32 **If I no longer want a gift someone gave me, isn't it okay to get rid of it?:** This next section draws on my article "The Day I was Stumped," *Love Unleashes Life* blog, March 30, 2016, https://loveunleasheslife.com/blog/2016/3/30/the-day-i-was-stumped -by-stephanie-gray.

35 **"Love is the ultimate and the highest goal":** Viktor Frankl, *Man's Search for Meaning* (New York: Pocket Books, 1985), 57.

35 **an exchange Sergeant Briggs had with a man wanting to jump off the bridge:** Briggs, *Guardian of the Golden Gate*, 273.

CHAPTER 3

38   **the Grants:** Not their real names.

41   **proving the existence of God:** Philosopher Peter Kreeft has written extensively on the topic of the existence of God. Learn more at https://www.peterkreeft.com/.

45   **"When peace like a river attendeth my way":** Horatio Spafford, "It Is Well with My Soul," https://www.spaffordhymn.com/.

45   **dialogue between Jesus and Little James:** *The Chosen*, directed by Dallas Jenkins (Angel Studios / Loaves & Fishes, 2017–), season 3, episode 2.

46   **"Any God who would heal one person and let another die":** Eric Metaxas, *Miracles: What They Are, Why They Happen, and How They Can Change Your Life* (New York: Penguin, 2014), 61.

46   **"If God *always* answered our prayers as we wanted him to":** Metaxas, 61–63.

47   **"It took three of the greatest heartaches I could bear":** Amber VanVickle, "A Mother Finds Love at the Foot of the Cross," *National Catholic Register*, May 12, 2018, https://www.ncregister.com/blog/a-mother-finds-love-at-the-foot-of-the-cross.

48   **"Perhaps the Lord is telling us":** Amber VanVickle, "When the Miracle Doesn't Come," *National Catholic Register*, June 15, 2019, https://www.ncregister.com/blog/when -the-miracle-doesn-t-come.

48   **"I used to want the longest life":** WildGooseTV, "Rebuild My Faith—Finding God in the midst of suffering with Dave and Amber VanVickle," YouTube video, February 27, 2023, https://www.youtube.com/watch?v=U39GTT6rt4U.

49   **"The doctors tell us there is nothing more they can do":** Amber VanVickle, post on "Support the VanVickles in their fight with cancer," GoFundMe, https://www .gofundme.com/f/ss63vd-support-the-vanvickles-in-their-fight-with-cancer.

49   **"Today the world is full of doubting Thomases":** Catherine Doherty, from *Season of Mercy* (1996), 127–129, reprinted in *Restoration Newspaper of Madonna House*, April 2023, 4–5.

51   **our new "heartsong":** "Heartsong" is a word used by Mattie Stepanek, an inspiring young boy whose story is told in a later chapter.

54   **"What if your blessings come through raindrops?":** Laura Story, *When God Doesn't Fix It: Lessons You Never Wanted to Learn, Truths You Can't Live Without* (Nashville, TN: W Publishing, 2015), 224, 226, 236.

54   **"Life is filled with things you don't expect":** "Interview with Laura Story," CBN 700 Club, https://cmsedit.cbn.com/700club/laura-story.

54   **"in order to unleash love in the human person":** John Paul II, *Salvifici Doloris* 29, apostolic letter, February 11, 1984, vatican.va.

57   **Rick Hoyt:** Learn about the Hoyts at https://teamhoyt.com/.

57   **after his recovery he was back to running with his son:** IRONMAN Triathlon, "Dick & Rick Hoyt," YouTube video, February 5, 2007, https://www.youtube.com/watch?v=dDnrLv6z-mM.

58   **Jimmy V Perseverance Award acceptance speeches:** "The Story of Team Hoyt @ ESPY's 2013—Jimmy V Perseverance Award," YouTube video, July 19, 2013, https://www.youtube.com/watch?v=xBXy1EH4nYc.

58   **Justin Skeesuck and Patrick Gray:** Learn about their story at https://www.pushinc.us/about.

58   ***I'll Push You: Embracing God's Promise of Provision***: I'll Push You, "I'll Push You: Embracing God's Promise of Provision," YouTube video, March 15, 2016, https://youtube/NfQpfi8qsR0.

59   **Claudia's story:** "I'll Push You."

62   **"What do you get from loss?":** Stephen Colbert, Interview on *Anderson Cooper 360°*, August 15, 2019, https://twitter.com/AC360/status/1162183695270387712.

CHAPTER 4

64   **An encounter science predicted would never happen:** This section is taken from my article "Comfortable in His Skin," *Love Unleashes Life* blog, February 3, 2017, https://loveunleasheslife.com/blog/2017/2/3/comfortable-in-his-skin-by-stephanie-gray.

64   **Moe Tapp:** Learn more about Moe at https://vimeo.com/86757114.

64 **Jonathan Pitre:** "'Butterfly Boy' Jonathan Pitre Recovering After Stem Cell Treatment," CTV News, September 9, 2016, http://www.ctvnews.ca/health/butterfly -boy-jonathan-pitre-recovering-after-stem-cell-treatment-1.3065188.

64 **"the worst disease you've never heard of":** Learn more about EB at http://www .debra.org/. That quote is used under the section "About EB."

68 **"When you see only death as a solution":** Advokate Life & Education Services, "Euthanasia in Canada? The Coming World of Assisted Dying," YouTube video, March 4, 2015, https://www.youtube.com/watch?v=SCKVqnO4n2U.

69 **letting nature take its course while offering comfort that addresses the whole person:** This section is taken from a booklet I wrote for The Chilliwack Pro-Life Society, *An FAQ about Euthanasia and Assisted Suicide*, available at https://loveunleasheslife.com/s /Euthanasia-FAQ.pdf.

69 **"Palliative care is an approach that":** "WHO Definition of Palliative Care," World Health Organization website, accessed November 22, 2023, https://www.who.int/cancer /palliative/definition/en/.

69 **"With 26 years' experience as a palliative care nurse":** Jean Echlin, in "How Will You Say Goodbye to Someone You Love?" Euthanasia Prevention Coalition, January 2006.

71 **"I think it is possible for people to have a 'good' death":** Julia Bright, "Live Every Stage Fully," *Love Unleashes Life* blog, November 22, 2016, https://loveunleasheslife.com /blog/2016/11/22/live-every-stage-fully-by-dr-julia-bright.

72 **"Since dying is a necessary part of life":** TED, "What Really Matters at the End of Life," YouTube video, September 30, 2015, https://www.youtube.com/watch?v=apb SsILLh28&t=80s.

73 **"Let death be what takes us, not lack of imagination":** "What Really Matters at the End of Life."

73 **"I would like to challenge each of you today":** Bright, "Live Every Stage Fully."

75 **Barry and Izzy Sim:** Andrew Dowdell and Kate Schneider, "Barry Sim and His Wife Izzy Sim Missed Flight Malaysia Airlines Flight MH17," *News.com.au*, July 18, 2014, https://www.news.com.au/travel/travel-updates/incidents/barry-sim-and-his-wife-izzy -sim-missed-flight-malaysia-airlines-flight-mh17/news-story/c64eb963a55ae6c11 ed63c91dbc04d38.

76   **"nine out of ten people who attempt suicide and survive will not go on to die by suicide at a later date":** "Attempters' Longterm Survival," Harvard T.H. Chan School of Public Health website, accessed November 22, 2023, https://www.hsph.harvard.edu /means-matter/means-matter/survival/.

76   **"The millisecond my hands left the rail—instantaneous regret":** Kevin Hines Story, "I Jumped Off the Golden Gate Bridge—Podcast with Steven Sulley," YouTube video, August 14, 2023, https://www.youtube.com/watch?v=ysEQV0lZvBo&t=770s.

77   **Kevin Hines:** Learn more about Kevin's remarkable story of resilience at www.kevin hinesstory.com/.

79   **"Some of the possible burdens that may need to be considered":** Tadeusz Pacholczyk, "Going Too Far with DNR?" *Making Sense of Bioethics*, April 2013, https:// www.fathertad.com/files/9414/6917/1584/MSOB094_Going_Too_Far_with_DNR.pdf.

81   **"A patient in the last stages of stomach cancer":** "Q&A from the USCCB Committee on Doctrine and Committee on Pro-Life Activities regarding the Holy See's Responses on Nutrition and Hydration for Patients in a 'Vegetative State,'" United States Conference of Catholic Bishops website, https://www.usccb.org/issues-and-action/human -life-and-dignity/end-of-life/euthanasia/upload/q-a-nutrition-and-hydration-patients -vegetative-state.pdf.

81   **"In some cases, feeding tubes may actually cause significant problems of their own":** Tadeusz Pacholczyk, "Are Feeding Tubes Required?" *Making Sense of Bioethics*, December 2006, https://www.fathertad.com/files/8014/7025/5378/MSOB_018_Are _Feeding_Tubes_Required.pdf.

82   **Terri Schiavo:** Learn more at https://terrischiavo.org/.

83   **the principle of double effect:** *Principles of Medical Ethics*, MODULE 2-2 Readings, National Catholic Bioethics Center, National Certification Program in Health Care Ethics (course handout from 2008–2009 year).

85   **Calvary Hospital in New York:** "About Calvary Hospital," Calvary Hospital website, accessed November 22, 2023, https://www.calvaryhospital.org/about/.

85   **the Brescia-Cimino arterio-venous fistula:** "Meet Our Team," Calvary Hospital website, accessed November 22, 2023, https://www.calvaryhospital.org/about/meet-our -team/michael-j-brescia-md/.

85   **releasing his invention immediately instead of handing it over to a drug company:** "Dr. Brescia: An Interview with Sr. Mary Margaret Hope, SV," *Imprint*, Spring 2017 issue, https://sistersoflife.org/wp-content/uploads/2019/05/SV-Imprint-Spring-2017.pdf.

85   **"At Calvary, we have never, ever, in any way, hastened death purposely":** "Dr. Brescia: An Interview with Sr. Mary Margaret Hope, SV."

CHAPTER 5

86   **"The greatest disease in the West today is not TB or leprosy":** Teresa of Kolkata, in *Mother Teresa: A Simple Path*, ed. Lucinda Vardey (New York: Ballantine Books, 1995), 79.

86   **Grace's story:** Taken from my article "An Encounter with Grace," *Love Unleashes Life* blog, April 12, 2017, https://loveunleasheslife.com/blog/2017/4/12/an-encounter-with-grace-by-stephanie-gra.

89   **"The moment we label suicide an act of dignity":** Christopher Stefanick, "Death with Dignity," YouTube video, January 6, 2015, https://www.youtube.com/watch?t=66&v=0nf_rb2qkbE.

89   **"the quality or state of being worthy, honored, or esteemed":** *Merriam-Webster Dictionary Online*, s.v. "Dignity," accessed July 22, 2020, https://www.merriam-webster.com/dictionary/dignity.

90   **a Parisian apartment being untouched for decades:** Leon Watson, "Inside the Paris Apartment Untouched for 70 Years: Treasure Trove Finally Revealed after Owner Locked Up and Fled at Outbreak of WWII," *Daily Mail*, May 12, 2013, https://www.dailymail.co.uk/news/article-2323297/Inside-Paris-apartment-untouched-70-years-Treasure-trove-finally-revealed-owner-locked-fled-outbreak-WWII.html.

91   **Martin Pistorius:** Learn more about Martin at http://www.martinpistorius.com/tmpsite/#home and https://twitter.com/martinpistorius?lang=en.

93   **"Virna looked at me properly":** Martin Pistorius, *Ghost Boy: The Miraculous Escape of a Misdiagnosed Boy Trapped Inside His Own Body* (Nashville, TN: Nelson Books, 2013), 21, 55.

94   **"The one person I talked to was God":** Pistorius, 182.

CHAPTER 6

97   he **"wasn't alone"**: Henry Fraser, *The Little Big Things: A Young Man's Belief that Every Day Can Be a Good Day* (London: Seven Dials, 2017), 15.

97   **"With the love of others, whoever they are, you can face darkness"**: Fraser, 20.

97   **"It was as if their tears"**: Fraser, 27.

98   **see Ove with new eyes**: This section is drawn from my article "The Secondary Emotion of Anger," *Love Unleashes Life* blog, February 18, 2019, https://loveunleasheslife .com/blog/2019/2/18/the-secondary-emotion-of-anger-by-stephanie-gray.

99   **"I want you, John! I want you!"**: *Walk the Line*, directed by James Mangold (Fox 2000 Pictures, 2005).

99   **"Why is it that people who have so little and have suffered so much seem to be happier?"**: Warren Berger, *A More Beautiful Question: The Power of Inquiry to Spark Breakthrough Ideas* (New York: Bloomsbury, 2014), 191.

101   **"Happiness [is] only real when shared"**: Rachel Heller and Amir Levine, *Attached: The New Science of Adult Attachment and How It Can Help You Find—and Keep—Love* (New York: Penguin, 2011), 110.

101   **"Canada's Loneliest People"**: Meagan Campbell, "Canada's Loneliest People: 25 Per Cent of Canadian Seniors Live Alone, but There Lies a Little Documented Population within That Demographic That Live in Acute Isolation," *Maclean's Magazine*, June 22, 2018, https://www.macleans.ca/society/canadas-loneliest-people/.

102   **"One patient, who still has children and no serious medical concerns"**: Campbell, "Canada's Loneliest People."

102   **"ended her daily walks, library visits and all the activities"**: Avis Favaro, Elizabeth St. Philip, and Alexandra Mae Jones, "Facing Another Retirement Home Lockdown, 90-Year-Old Chooses Medically Assisted Death," CTV News, November 19, 2020, https://www.ctvnews.ca/health/facing-another-retirement-home-lockdown-90 -year-old-chooses-medically-assisted-death-1.5197140.

102   **"more concrete medical health" issues**: Favaro, St. Philip, and Jones, "Facing Another Retirement Home Lockdown."

103   **"She just truly did not believe"**: Favaro, St. Philip, and Jones, "Facing Another Retirement Home Lockdown."

CHAPTER 7

106 "He wasn't a very good husband": ABC News In-depth, "This Old Man Is Healthy But Wants to Kill Himself," YouTube video, July 18, 2018, https://www.youtube.com/watch?v=tWDnW17-gNk.

106 unfit to work on campus: Laura Gartry, "David Goodall: Australia's Oldest Working Scientist Fights to Stay at University," ABC News, August 26, 2016, https://www.abc.net.au/news/2016-08-27/david-goodall:-australias-oldest-working-scientist/7788844.

106 he fell at home: Charlotte Hamlyn, "The Final Move," ABC News, May 4, 2018, https://www.abc.net.au/news/2018-05-05/david-goodall-trip-to-switzerland-for-voluntary-euthanasia/9716354.

106 "What's the use of that?": Sheena McKenzie, Melissa Bell, Saskya Vandoorne, and Ben Westcott, "104-Year-Old Scientist David Goodall 'Welcomes Death' at Swiss Clinic," CNN, May 9, 2018, https://www.cnn.com/2018/05/08/health/david-goodall-australia-switzerland-interview-intl/index.html.

106 "I am not happy. I want to die": Lindsey Bever, "David Goodall, 104, Just Took His Own Life after Making a Powerful Statement about Assisted Death," *The Washington Post*, May 10, 2018, https://www.washingtonpost.com/news/to-your-health/wp/2018/05/09/this-104-year-old-plans-to-die-tomorrow-and-hopes-to-change-views-on-assisted-suicide/.

107 "was full of life": "This Old Man Is Healthy But Wants to Kill Himself."

107 "Well, it's mainly the people here": "This Old Man Is Healthy But Wants to Kill Himself."

108 "All of us have common needs to be recognized": "What Happens When a Nursing Home and a Day Care Center Share a Roof?" PBS News Hour, May 10, 2016, https://www.pbs.org/newshour/show/what-happens-when-a-nursing-home-and-a-day-care-center-share-a-roof.

108 my friend Kathleen: This and the next story are taken from my article "A Resolution for the New Year: In the Face of Suffering, Unleash Love," *Love Unleashes Life* blog, January 4, 2017, https://loveunleasheslife.com/blog/2017/1/3/a-resolution-for-the-new-year-in-the-face-of-someones-suffering-unleash-your-love-by-stephanie-gray.

109   my three-month-old nephew Carl: This section is taken from my article "The Circle of Life," *Love Unleashes Life* blog, December 5, 2016, https://loveunleasheslife.com /blog/2016/12/5/the-circle-of-life-by-stephanie-gray.

112   "Silence is difficult, but it enables man to let himself be led by God": Robert Sarah, *The Power of Silence: Against the Dictatorship of Noise* (San Francisco: Ignatius, 2017), 54, 69.

CHAPTER 8

116   "if for whatever reason she was no longer judged to be of sound mind": "A Nurse's Story: Euthanasia (MAiD) Death Was Not Dignified," Euthanasia Prevention Coalition blog, May 4, 2023, https://alexschadenberg.blogspot.com/2023/05/a-nurses -story-euthanasia-maid-death.html.

116   "confused and groggy": "A Nurse's Story."

116   "unable to properly confirm she wanted the euthanasia": "A Nurse's Story."

121   "Today is the day *I have chosen* to pass away": TODAY, "Brittany Maynard's Husband Tells Megyn Kelly About Her Decision To Die | Megyn Kelly TODAY," YouTube video, June 1, 2018, https://www.youtube.com/watch?v=itihpltdVec. Emphasis added.

121   Her husband framed things this way: "Brittany Maynard's Husband Tells Megyn Kelly About Her Decision To Die."

123   "We're divorced from my father because he did some mean and scary things to us": "Mattie Stepanek on Larry King Live," YouTube video, July 7, 2014, https://www .youtube.com/watch?v=D3ALna5Kg_M&t=583s.

123   the full-length interview of him on *Larry King Live*: "Mattie Stepanek on Larry King Live."

124   doctors were convinced he was weeks or even days away from dying: EWTN, "World Over—Jeni Stepanek on Mattie Stepanek's Cause for Sainthood with Raymond Arroyo," YouTube video, July 20, 2018, https://www.youtube.com/watch?v =DBUNIvbtkkI.

125   "I have to live until the moment I die": "Jeni Stepanek on Mattie Stepanek's Cause for Sainthood with Raymond Arroyo."

125 **"We have known kings and queens":** "About Mattie," Mattie Matters website, http://mattiematters.org/about-mattie/.

125 **"Mattie would be the single biggest relationship that ever developed out of a show":** OWN, "#24: Meeting Mattie Stepanek | TV Guide's Top 25 | Oprah Winfrey Network," YouTube video, August 29, 2012, https://www.youtube.com/watch?v=3mas TPPXfIU.

125 **"one of the sweetest souls I have ever known":** OWN, "How Mattie Stepanek's Words Inspired Millions | The Oprah Winfrey Show | Oprah Winfrey Network," YouTube video, June 22, 2014, https://www.youtube.com/watch?v=ZxD-U1rY0vw.

125 **"He seemed to know God rather than learn about God":** EWTN, "World Over—JeniStepanekandDr.DeniseHunnellwithRaymondArroyo—09-01-2011,"YouTube video, September 2, 2011, https://www.youtube.com/watch?v=1EeR4DPr9LQ&t=926s.

125 **"It's within a week of his death and he starts calling out, 'Nurse, nurse!'":** "Jeni Stepanek and Dr. Denise Hunnell with Raymond Arroyo."

126 **"The most meaningful and truly best of life":** John O'Leary, "The Best Flight I Ever Missed," John O'Leary Live Inspired website, February 24, 2020, http://johnoleary inspires.com/2020/02/the-best-flight-i-ever-missed/?mc_cid=b64bb30dc7&mc _eid=95492dac89.

127 **"Many of us labor under the illusion that control is always good":** Elisabeth Kübler-Ross and David Kessler, *Life Lessons: Two Experts on Death and Dying Teach Us About the Mysteries of Life and Living* (New York: Scribner, 2000), 186–187.

CHAPTER 9

128 **"We are caught in an inescapable network of mutuality":** Martin Luther King Jr., "Letter from a Birmingham Jail," April 16, 1963, https://www.africa.upenn.edu /Articles_Gen/Letter_Birmingham.html.

128 **Choices we make have a permeating influence:** This section is drawn from my article "The Impact of Choices," *Love Unleashes Life* blog, January 12, 2017, https:// loveunleasheslife.com/blog/2017/1/12/the-impact-of-choices-by-stephanie-gray.

128 **paying it forward:** Tina Chen, "Starbucks Customers Break 1,000 in Pay-It-Forward Record," ABC News, December 27, 2013, https://abcnews.go.com/blogs/headlines/2013 /12/starbucks-customers-break-1000-in-pay-it-forward-record/.

129   "One boy was about to take his own life": James Dunn, "Woman Born with No Arms or Legs Reveals Her Empowering Fight Against Bullies, Abusers and Suicidal Thoughts to Become an Inspiration to Thousands in Colombia," *Daily Mail*, July 28, 2015, https://www.dailymail.co.uk/news/article-3177324/Woman-born-no-arms-legs-reveals -empowering-fight-against-bullies-abusers-suicidal-thoughts-inspiration-thousands -Colombia.html.

129   David Dow recounts Will's story: David Dow, "Lessons from Death Row Inmates," TEDxAustin, February 2012, https://www.ted.com/talks/david_r_dow_lessons _from_death_row_inmates?language=en.

130   *Fatal Flaws* and *The Euthanasia Deception*: *Fatal Flaws: Legalising Assisted Death*, directed by Kevin Dunn (DunnMedia / Euthanasia Prevention Coalition, 2018); *The Euthanasia Deception*, directed by Kevin Dunn (DunnMedia / Euthanasia Prevention Coalition, 2016).

131   "In the pioneering years of Dutch euthanasia": Theo Boer, "Be Careful What You Wish for When You Legalize Active Killing," Euthanasia Prevention Coalition blog, October 5, 2020, https://alexschadenberg.blogspot.com/2020/10/be-careful-what-you -wish-for-when-you.html.

131   euthanasia was set to be expanded in the Netherlands: Andrew Mark Miller, "Netherlands Expands Euthanasia Laws to Include Terminally Ill Children as Young as 1-Year-Old," Fox News, April 26, 2023, https://www.foxnews.com/world/netherlands -expands-euthanasia-laws-include-terminally-ill-children-young-as-1-year-old.

131   one of the most liberal assisted suicide laws in the world: Gus Alexiou, "Canada's New Euthanasia Laws Carry Upsetting Nazi-Era Echoes, Warns Expert," *Forbes*, August 15, 2022, https://www.forbes.com/sites/gusalexiou/2022/08/15/canadas-new-euthanasia- laws-carry-upsetting-nazi-era-echoes-warns-expert/?sh=519bdacbc7b8; Paul Wells, "'This Is a Big Step in Canadian Society and Justice,' Trudeau Says of Assisted Dying Bill," *The Star,* June 7, 2016, https://www.thestar.com/news/canada/2016/06/07/trudeau-down plays-seriousness-of-missing-bill-c-14-deadline-wells.html.

131   Consider the many ways Canada is already standing out: "MAiD," End of Life Law and Policy in Canada website, http://eol.law.dal.ca/?page_id=2472.

132   "the requirement for a person's natural death to be reasonably foreseeable": Department of Justice Canada, "New Medical Assistance in Dying Legislation Becomes Law," Government of Canada website, March 17, 2021, https://www.canada.ca/en /department-justice/news/2021/03/new-medical-assistance-in-dying-legislation-becomes -law.html.

132   **"You do *not* need to have a fatal or terminal condition":** "Medical Assistance in Dying," Government of Canada website, https://www.canada.ca/en/health-canada /services/medical-assistance-dying.html.

132   **"persons suffering solely from a mental illness":** "Canada's Medical Assistance in Dying (MAID) Law," Government of Canada website, accessed November 22, 2023, https://www.justice.gc.ca/eng/cj-jp/ad-am/bk-di.html#e.

133   **suicide assistance for multiple chemical sensitivities:** Avis Favaro, "Woman with Chemical Sensitivities Chose Medically Assisted Death After Failed Bid to Get Better Housing," CTV News, August 24, 2022, https://www.ctvnews.ca/health/woman -with-chemical-sensitivities-chose-medically-assisted-death-after-failed-bid-to-get-better -housing-1.5860579.

133   **suicide assistance for hearing loss:** Flo Read, "'Why Did Canada Help My Brother Die'" *UnHerd*, October 18, 2022, https://unherd.com/2022/10/why-did-canada-help-my -brother-die/; Maria Cheng, "Experts Troubled by Canada's Euthanasia Laws," *Los Angeles Times*, August 11, 2022, latimes.com/world-nation/story/2022-08-11/disturbing -experts-troubled-by-canadas-euthanasia-laws.

133   **suicide assistance for diabetes:** The Fifth Estate, "Is it too easy to die in Canada? Surprising approvals for medically assisted death—The Fifth Estate," YouTube video, January 19, 2023, https://www.youtube.com/watch?v=plinQAHZRvk.

133   **suicide assistance for impoverished and disabled man:** "Is it too easy to die in Canada?"

133   **suicide assistance for patient dressed as clown:** Stefanie Green, "Assisted: A Doctor's Story of Assisting Death and Embracing Life," *Body+Soul*, April 1, 2022, https:// www.bodyandsoul.com.au/mind-body/assisted-a-doctors-story-of-assisting-death-and -embracing-life/news-story/b51870c8967a39d9fa0447f6b7ab94fc. This is an edited extract from Green's book by the same title.

135   **"I will not give a lethal drug to anyone if I am asked, nor will I advise such a plan":** "Greek Medicine: The Hippocratic Oath," National Library of Medicine website, accessed November 22, 2023, https://www.nlm.nih.gov/hmd/greek/greek_oath.html.

135   **when actor Robin Williams committed suicide in 2014:** "Suicides Spiked After Death of Robin Williams," Columbia University Mailman School of Public Health website, February 7, 2018, https://www.publichealth.columbia.edu/news/suicides-spiked -after-death-robin-williams#:~:text=In%20the%20months%20after%20Robin,to%20 44%20were%20particularly%20affected.

135   **"Responsible reporting by the media is an essential component of suicide prevention":** *National Suicide Prevention Strategies: Progress, Examples, Indicators* (Geneva: World Health Organization, 2018), 9, https://iris.who.int/bitstream/handle/10665/279765 /9789241515016-eng.pdf?sequence=1.

135   **other people suffering with her same condition have also expressed interest:** Favaro, "Woman with Chemical Sensitivities Chose Medically Assisted Death After Failed Bid to Get Better Housing."

136   **Since MAID's legalization in Canada, assisted suicide has been steadily increasing:** "Third Annual Report on Medical Assistance in Dying in Canada 2021," Government of Canada website, https://www.canada.ca/en/health-canada/services/medical -assistance-dying/annual-report-2021.html#a3.1.

136   **The Netherlands has also seen an increase in such deaths:** "A Critical Look at the Rising Euthanasia Rates in the Netherlands," *Healthcare in Europe*, January 15, 2021, https:// healthcare-in-europe.com/en/news/a-critical-look-at-the-rising-euthanasia-rates-in-the -netherlands.html#:~:text=Official%20data%20show%20that%20the,just%20over%20 4%25%20in%202019.

136   **John O'Leary:** John O'Leary, *On Fire: The 7 Choices to Ignite a Radically Inspired Life* (New York: Gallery Books, 2016), 166.

137   **"Jack Buck changed my life":** O'Leary, 166.

137   **Jack had not been a friend of the O'Learys before the fire:** O'Leary, 170–171.

138   **"If he was a horse, I'd shoot him":** John O'Leary, "Saved from the Fire," Beliefnet, accessed November 22, 2023, https://www.beliefnet.com/inspiration/articles/john-oleary -saved-from-the-fire.aspx.

138   **"live inspired":** Learn more at https://johnolearyinspires.com/.

CHAPTER 10

139   **"A man should hear a little music":** Goethe, quoted in *Musical Mosaics: A Collection of Six Hundred Selections from Musical Literature, Ancient and Modern. Including Extracts from Many Later Critical and Aesthetical Writings*, ed. W.F. Gates (Philadelphia: Theo Presser, 1889), 95.

140   **"beauty will save the world":** Fyodor Dostoyevsky, *The Idiot*, part 3, chapter 5.

142 **"Hope is like a bird that senses the dawn and carefully starts to sing even while it is still dark":** This is quoted throughout the internet and has been attributed as "unknown" or "anonymous," but a similar version of it is said by Rabindranath Tagore in the book *Fireflies*: "Faith is the bird that feels the light and sings when the dawn is still dark."

142 **Alive Inside:** *Alive Inside: A Story of Music and Memory*, directed by Michael Rossato-Bennett (Projector Media / The Shelley & Donald Rubin Foundation, 2014).

142 **"Our vision is to give unprecedented support to seniors to be all they can be":** "About Us," Fit Minds website, accessed November 22, 2023, https://fitminds.ca/vision -mission/.

146 **case of a woman cooking a yam over a fire:** Paul Brand and Philip Yancey, *The Gift of Pain: Why We Hurt & What We Can Do About It* (Grand Rapids, MI: Zondervan, 1997), 6.

147 **"Dr. Brand, these are not good hands":** Brand and Yancey, 135.

147 **"My stomach twisted in a knot as John told me of the rejection he had encountered":** Brand and Yancey, 135–137.

149 **"Margaret saw a vivid illustration of the kind of abuse that can happen":** Brand and Yancey, 146.

149 **"It involved detaching one end of part of the temporalis muscle":** Brand and Yancey, 146.

149 **"cat breeder":** Brand and Yancey, 127–128.

151 **"The touch of the Master's hand":** Myra Brooks Welch, "The Touch of the Master's Hand," 1921, https://allpoetry.com/Myra-Brooks-Welch.

EPILOGUE

152 **"Some people come into our lives and quickly go":** Shelly Markham et al., *Flavia and the Dream Maker: The Musical* (Woodstock, IL: Dramatic, 2004), 23.

164 **"There are places in the heart that do not yet exist":** Léon Bloy, quoted in Phil Small, *On the Way to Here: Reflections on Things That Matter* (Australia: Friesen, 2017), 115.